THAILAND

TRAVEL GUIDE

The Ultimate Book To Discovering The Best Of Thailand

Peterson Brian

Table of Contents

Brief History

Thailand, famed for its rich cultural heritage, breathtaking landscapes, and bustling cities, possesses an intriguing history that has formed the nation into what it is today. Spanning thousands of years, the history of Thailand is a tapestry woven with influences from indigenous civilizations, neighboring kingdoms, and global trade.

The earliest evidence of human occupation in the region dates back to roughly 3600 BCE, with signs of farming and metalworking found in archaeological sites. These early settlers established the groundwork for what would later become the Thai civilization.

One of the major historical influences in Thailand was the establishment of the Khmer Empire, based in present-day Cambodia. The Khmer Empire's influence spread into portions of Thailand, leaving behind architectural marvels like the iconic Angkor Wat temple complex. As the Khmer Empire waned, many city-states and kingdoms developed in the Thai region.

The Sukhothai Kingdom, formed in the 13th century, is commonly regarded as the origin of Thai civilization. It adopted Theravada Buddhism and established the foundation for the Siamese culture that would evolve. The kingdom is recognized for its administrative changes, art, and different sculpting styles.

The Ayutthaya Kingdom succeeded Sukhothai, flourishing from the 14th to the 18th century. Ayutthaya became a significant commerce center, attracting merchants from throughout Asia and Europe. This period saw the rise of a great maritime empire, with Ayutthaya playing a crucial role in regional trade and diplomacy.

However, Ayutthaya's prosperity was damaged by the Burmese invasion in the mid-18th century. The city was ransacked and left in ruins. This represented a turning moment in Thai history, leading to the rise of the Thonburi Kingdom under King Taksin. His rule was short-lived, but it prepared the foundation for the Chakri Dynasty's march to prominence.

The Chakri Dynasty, established in 1782 by King Rama I, remains the royal house of Thailand until this day. The dynasty is recognized for its efforts to modernize the country, including administrative changes, infrastructure development, and diplomatic connections with Western powers. King Rama IV and King Rama V furthered these reforms, guaranteeing Thailand's sovereignty in the face of colonial pressures.

The 20th century offered hardships as Thailand went through two World Wars. It succeeded in keeping its independence, but not without enduring internal political battles and military coups. The country formally changed its name from Siam to Thailand in 1939 to underline its national identity.

During the latter half of the 20th century, Thailand saw tremendous economic expansion, particularly during the 1980s and 1990s. The country embraced industrialization and became a global powerhouse for manufacturing and tourism. Its modernizing initiatives were, however, accompanied by social and political obstacles.

Today, Thailand stands as a lively and diversified nation, conserving its cultural past while embracing modernity. Its history, a blend of indigenous influences and interactions with neighboring civilizations, has formed a unique tapestry that appeals to travelers seeking a deeper understanding of its past.

Conclusion

The history of Thailand is a thrilling voyage through time, defined by the rise and fall of kingdoms, cultural exchanges, and a constant pursuit of national identity. From its early prehistoric settlements to the founding of mighty empires and its modern metamorphosis, Thailand's history is a story of persistence, adaptation, and growth. Tourists traveling the country have the opportunity to immerse themselves in this rich tapestry, seeing firsthand the legacy of the past that continues to shape the present.

Geography

Thailand boasts a diversified geography that contains lush forests, mountain ranges, fertile plains, and stunning coastlines. Its geography substantially influences its climate, biodiversity, and cultural development.

Situated in the middle of the Indochina Peninsula, Thailand is bordered by Myanmar to the west, Laos to the north, and Cambodia to the southeast, and Malaysia to the south. Its shoreline along the Gulf of Thailand and the Andaman Sea contributes to its strategic maritime significance. The country can be largely split into four geographical regions: the Central Plains, the Northern Highlands, the Northeastern Plateau, and the Southern Peninsula.

Starting with the Central Plains, this region is characterized by the Chao Phraya River, which is the lifeblood of Thailand. The river system aids agriculture and transport, supporting rice paddies and various ecosystems. The lush floodplain is home to Bangkok, the busy capital city, which has historically been a vital economic and cultural hub.

Moving north, the Northern Highlands feature mountain ranges including the Shan Hills and the Phi Pan Nam Range. These elevation locations contribute to a milder climate and are noted for their biodiversity. The city of Chiang Mai, tucked in this region, is a center for cultural heritage and ecotourism. The scenery here ranges from deep forests to terraced rice fields cultivated by hill people.

In the Northeastern Plateau, or Isan, a more dry and less populous region, you find the Khorat Plateau. This region is significant for agriculture and, historically, has been a crucial rice-producing area. Its terrain and climate have affected the largely agrarian lifestyle of its residents.

The Southern Peninsula is defined by a small land strip connecting to Malaysia. The southern region is characterized by a magnificent coastline, pristine beaches, and several islands in the Andaman Sea and the Gulf of Thailand. Phuket, Krabi, and Koh Samui are some of the prominent tourist sites located here. The southern terrain also includes the harsh Tenasserim Hills and the Malayan Peninsula.

Thailand's location considerably influences its climate, which is tropical and influenced by the monsoon season. The monsoon winds bring considerable rains to many sections of the country throughout the wet season, impacting agriculture and overall everyday life.

Biodiversity is another outstanding characteristic of Thailand's geography. Its various settings sustain a broad assortment of flora and wildlife, both on land and in water. The country is home to many national parks and wildlife reserves, conserving habitats for elephants, tigers, gibbons, and a profusion of bird species. The mangrove forests along coastal areas provide critical breeding grounds for aquatic life.

Conclusion
Thailand's geography is a tapestry of intricate landscapes, each with its unique qualities and influences. The country's rivers, mountains, plains, and coasts shape its climate, culture, and wildlife. From the busy urban sprawl of Bangkok to the serene beauty of the northern highlands and the stunning beaches in the south, Thailand's topography is a

treasure trove that continues to amaze and inspire both its people and visitors from across the world.

Tourists Must Know Things Before Visiting

Before departing on your journey to Thailand, it's necessary to be well-prepared with essential information to guarantee a smooth and pleasurable vacation. Here's an overview of what every tourist should know before visiting Thailand.

Visa Requirements
Most tourists can enter Thailand without a visa for up to 30 days, depending on their nationality. However, if you plan to remain longer, you'll need to apply for a tourist visa in advance. Ensure you understand the visa requirements and duration before your travel.

Currency and Payments
The native currency is the Thai Baht (THB). While credit cards are generally accepted in urban areas, it's important to carry cash, especially in rural regions and street markets. ATMs are generally available, but some may impose exorbitant withdrawal fees.

Culture and Etiquette
Respect for Thai culture is of the highest importance. When visiting temples, dress modestly, covering your shoulders and knees. Remove your shoes before visiting sacred locations. The traditional greeting is the "wai," a modest bow with hands pushed together. Avoid touching people's heads, as the head is regarded as the most sacred portion of the body.

Local Laws and Customs
Thailand has tight regulations regarding drugs, and punishments for drug-related offenses are high. Disrespecting the monarchy is likewise a punishable offense. Public shows of affection should be kept modest, and it's necessary to be cognizant of local norms and traditions.

Health and Safety
Consult your doctor about essential immunizations before flying to Thailand. Be cautious with tap water; it's advisable to consume bottled or boiling water. Mosquito-borne infections like dengue fever are frequent, so take insect repellent. Traffic in Thailand can be chaotic, so use caution when crossing roadways.

Bargaining
Bargaining is widespread in marketplaces and street vendors. Approach it as a friendly interaction rather than a confrontation. Start with a lesser price and work your way up until both sides agree.

Electricity
The normal voltage is 220V, and the plugs are commonly two-pronged flat or circular sockets. You might need an adaptor based on your native country's plug type.

Healthcare and Insurance
While Thailand offers great medical facilities, it's necessary to have comprehensive travel insurance that covers medical bills. Check if your insurance includes activities like motorbike riding, as accidents are rather prevalent among tourists.

SIM Cards and Communication
Getting a local SIM card upon arrival is important for keeping connected and accessing data during your trip. There are multiple providers offering prepaid SIM cards with varying data bundles.

Cultural Sensitivity
Thailand is a largely Buddhist country, and its religious traditions and symbols are deeply valued. Refrain from touching or climbing on monuments, and maintain a respectful distance during religious ceremonies.

Environmental Responsibility
Thailand's natural beauty is a big appeal for travelers. Help safeguard the environment by avoiding single-use plastics, engaging in beach cleanups, and following appropriate trekking and wildlife-watching techniques.

Time Zone
Thailand follows Indochina Time (ICT), which is UTC+7. Be careful of the time difference while making travel reservations or arranging activities.

Tipping Etiquette
Tipping isn't typical in Thailand, however, it's appreciated for great service. In restaurants, rounding up the bill is common. If a service charge is included, additional tipping might not be necessary.

Booking Accommodation
Thailand offers a wide range of accommodations, from affordable hostels to luxurious resorts. Research choices depending on your tastes and reserve in advance, especially during peak tourist seasons.

Responsible Tourism

Support local communities through purchasing at local markets, staying at locally-owned lodgings, and engaging in community-based tourist programs. Avoid acts that abuse animals or contribute to environmental deterioration.

Emergency Numbers

In case of crises, the general emergency number in Thailand is 191 (police) and 1669 (ambulance and rescue). It's also a good idea to have the contact details of your embassy or consulate.

Conclusion

Thailand's attractiveness rests in its various scenery, kind hospitality, and fascinating culture. By familiarizing yourself with these crucial components before your trip, you can ensure a more enriching and delightful experience. Whether you're touring ancient temples, sunbathing on pristine beaches, or enjoying exquisite cuisine, adopting the rituals and practices of Thailand will definitely improve your adventure and leave you with lasting memories.

Best Touring Apps and websites

To make the most of your vacation to Thailand, utilizing dependable touring websites is crucial, here, you'll find a full analysis of these websites, along with pertinent links to help you organize your trip effectively, here are some of the top ones:

Tourism Authority of Thailand (TAT)
The official website administered by the Thai government gives a plethora of information. From immigration requirements to location guides, TAT provides a comprehensive resource for tourists. Their site provides details about cultural events, festivals, and recommended itineraries.
www.tourismthailand.org/

TripAdvisor
This popular platform aggregates ratings and recommendations from tourists worldwide. You may get information on hotels, restaurants, attractions, and activities, along with traveler-submitted images and candid opinions.
www.tripadvisor.com/Tourism-g293915-Thailand-Vacations.html

Agoda
As one of Asia's biggest online travel agents, Agoda is ideal for booking hotels and accommodations. They frequently feature special bargains and a broad assortment of products across different price levels.
www.agoda.com/country/thailand.html

Booking.com

Another well-known booking platform, Booking.com, offers a vast choice of accommodations in Thailand, from hotels to guesthouses and hostels. Their user-friendly layout and flexible booking choices make it a popular pick.

www.booking.com/country/th.en-gb.html

Expedia

Expedia is an all-encompassing travel service that helps you book flights, hotels, car rentals, and even whole holiday packages. Their user-friendly design makes arranging your entire vacation straightforward and convenient.

www.expedia.com/Thailand.d178.Destination-Travel-Guides

Viator

If you're interested in tours and activities, Viator is a go-to website. They provide a wide range of possibilities, from cultural experiences to adventure activities, helping you explore Thailand's offerings in depth.

www.viator.com/Thailand/d20-ttd

Skyscanner

When it comes to finding flights, Skyscanner is a great tool. It compares flight costs from numerous airlines and travel agents to help you get the best bargains for your trip to Thailand.

www.skyscanner.net/flights-to/th/cheap-flights-to-thailand.html

Couchsurfing

If you want to connect with locals and discover Thailand from a new perspective, Couchsurfing allows you to stay with hosts who offer a spare room or sofa for tourists. It's a terrific approach to immerse oneself in the local culture.

www.couchsurfing.com/places/asia/thailand

Conclusion

Planning a vacation to Thailand becomes a simple process when you utilize these best touring websites. From official government information to user-generated evaluations, these platforms cover all elements of travel, including lodgings, flights, activities, and local insights. Remember to cross-reference information from numerous sources to verify accuracy and make informed decisions for your journey to the Land of Smiles.

Top Activities

Beyond its bustling cities, lively culture, and peaceful beaches, Thailand offers a wealth of outdoor activities for those seeking an adrenaline rush and a deeper connection with nature. From the foggy highlands in the north to the magnificent islands in the south, Thailand's various landscapes provide the perfect backdrop for a wide range of athletic outdoor activities. Here are some of the most thrilling outdoor excursions that await travelers in Thailand.

Water Sports

Thailand's magnificent coastal sceneries, crystal-clear waters, and tropical temperature make it a haven for water sports aficionados. With a myriad of activities accessible, ranging from tranquil to heart-pounding, Thailand offers a diverse and unique water sports experience.

Snorkeling and Scuba Diving

Thailand features some of the world's most known snorkeling and diving destinations, particularly in the Andaman Sea and the Gulf of Thailand. The Andaman side provides gems like the Similan Islands and Phi Phi Islands, where underwater enthusiasts can marvel at vivid coral reefs, unique marine life, and even shipwrecks. The Gulf of Thailand, on the other hand, is home to locations like Koh Tao, which is famed for its economical scuba diving training and diverse undersea terrain.

Kayaking and Canoeing

For those wanting a more quiet aquatic excursion, kayaking and canoeing through Thailand's placid waters provide a unique perspective of the country's natural splendor. One of the most renowned destinations is Phang Nga Bay, with its stunning limestone karsts towering from emerald waters. Additionally, the Ao Thalane mangrove forest in Krabi offers a maze of shallow rivers to explore, surrounded by lush flora and limestone cliffs.

Jet Skiing and Parasailing

For thrill-seekers, jet skiing and parasailing are popular activities provided at many of Thailand's beach resorts. Patong Beach in Phuket is recognized for its bustling water sports scene, including jet ski rentals and guided parasailing adventures. The adrenaline rush from skimming across the sea or soaring high above the coast is an amazing way to view Thailand's coastline.

Windsurfing and Kiteboarding

With constant winds and clean waves, Thailand's beaches provide a perfect location for windsurfing and kiteboarding.

Hua Hin is a prime site for these sports, offering rentals and tuition for all ability levels. The resort town's large sandy beaches and steady wind patterns make it a great site for gliding over the waves or performing acrobatic tricks with a kite.

White-Water Rafting
Away from the coastline, Thailand's rivers and rapids provide spectacular white-water rafting activities. Northern locations, such as Chiang Mai and Pai, present possibilities for maneuvering through tough rapids while surrounded by magnificent jungle surroundings. Mae Taeng River is a popular choice, with varied levels of difficulty ideal for both beginners and expert rafters.

Surfing
While Thailand may not be the first place that springs to mind for surfing, it nonetheless offers some decent waves for surf enthusiasts. Phuket's west coast, notably Kata Beach, delivers steady swells during the monsoon season, making it a preferred site for surfers of varying skill levels.

Wakeboarding and Water Skiing
For those who prefer balancing on a board, wakeboarding and waterskiing are popular choices in Thailand. Lakes like Lake Taco and Lake Maprang offer quiet and level waters, excellent for performing feats and maneuvers. These lakes also host tournaments and events, attracting both local and international water sports enthusiasts.

Underwater Walking
A unique aquatic pastime accessible in several Thai islands is underwater walking. Participants wear a helmet connected to an air hose, allowing them to walk over the ocean floor and

interact with marine life without the requirement for scuba diving certification. Coral Island and Koh Samui offer these experiences, offering individuals the ability to come up close to the aquatic world.

Rock Climbing

Thailand provides a wealth of climbing sites, each with its unique qualities and challenges. Some of the most notable places include Railay Beach, Ton Sai Beach, and Crazy Horse Buttress. These regions provide a variety of climbing methods, from limestone cliffs to overhangs, ensuring an amazing experience for climbers of all levels.

Climbing Seasons
The climbing seasons in Thailand are divided into two main periods - the dry season (November to February) and the hot season (March to May). The dry season gives great conditions for climbing due to the cold weather and lesser humidity. However, even during the hot season, climbers can still enjoy early morning or late afternoon sessions to avoid the extreme heat.

Climbing Grades

Thailand's climbing routes are graded using the French grading system. Ranging from 5a (easiest) to 9c (most difficult), climbers can choose routes that match their skill level. Beginners can find enough routes in the 5a to 6b range, while more experienced climbers can challenge themselves on climbs in the 6c to 8c range.

Climbing Styles

Thailand offers a choice of climbing methods to suit diverse inclinations. From bouldering to sport climbing and deep water soloing, climbers can enjoy a broad range of activities. Deep water soloing, in particular, is a unique sensation when climbers ascend cliffs over water, delivering a refreshing dip at the end of a successful climb.

Top Climbing Destinations

Railay Beach: This unique limestone peninsula is accessible only by boat due to its spectacular cliffs surrounding the mainland. Railay is recognized for its magnificent landscapes, crystal-clear lakes, and a wealth of climbing routes appropriate for all levels. Phra Nang Beach is famous for its classic paths and breathtaking views.

Ton Sai Beach: Adjacent to Railay, Ton Sai offers a more laid-back vibe and a tight-knit climbing culture. The area is noted for its adventurous routes and bustling backpacker culture. Climbers can enjoy a range of routes that appeal to different skill levels.

Crazy Horse Buttress: Located in Chiang Mai, Crazy Horse Buttress provides a different climbing experience compared to the coastal locations. The granite cliffs surrounded by lush forest give a unique backdrop for climbers. The colder environment here enables climbing even during the warmest months.

Logistics and Safety

Many climbing shops and schools are accessible near popular climbing spots, giving equipment rental, guided excursions, and climbing lessons for beginners. Safety is crucial, and climbers are encouraged to follow good safety protocols, wear suitable gear, and assess their own ability before tackling tough routes.

Cultural Respect

While enjoying the natural beauty of Thailand, climbers are asked to follow local customs and environmental rules. Treading carefully, abstaining from hurting the environment, and being aware of the local culture help sustain a happy connection between climbers and the community.

Hiking & Trekking

Hiking and trekking are two distinct hobbies that have a common thread of experiencing the outdoors on foot, however, they differ in intensity and duration. Hiking often refers to relatively shorter and less arduous excursions along well-maintained routes or trails. In comparison, trekking entails more arduous and extended excursions that often take several days and traverse through remote and hazardous terrain.

Thailand's diversified topography guarantees that both hiking and trekking experiences are abundantly available. In the northern section of the country, the region surrounding Chiang Mai is a hotspot for trekkers. The verdant woods, flowing waterfalls, and traditional hill tribe settlements provide a compelling background for multi-day treks. Popular routes include the Mae Hong Son Loop, which takes trekkers through stunning landscapes and offers insights into the local traditions of several ethnic groups.

Khao Sok National Park, located in southern Thailand, is a paradise for both hikers and trekkers. The park's old rainforests, limestone cliffs, and green lakes make a magnificent backdrop. Hikers can explore well-marked routes that lead to overlooks overlooking the picturesque Cheow Lan Lake, while trekkers can dive further into the forest on guided expeditions.

For those wanting an off-the-beaten-path excursion, the northern province of Nan provides a lesser-known though equally satisfying experience. The routes here cut through tranquil scenery, passing past terraced rice fields, traditional towns, and undisturbed wildness. This location provides a more private and tranquil ambiance for those wishing to escape the throngs often found in more popular trekking areas.

Timing your trekking or hiking excursion is key, as Thailand's climate can dramatically alter the experience. The cool and dry season, running from November to February, is often considered the finest period for outdoor activities. The weather is more temperate, making it pleasant for both trekking and hiking. On the other hand, the wet season, from June to October, brings significant rainfall, slick paths, and increased leech activity, making it less suited for these activities.

It's recommended to engage competent local guides who possess expertise in the terrain, weather conditions, and potential hazards. These guides can not only enhance your experience by providing insights into the local culture and nature but also secure your safety throughout the excursion.

Zip-lining

Zip-lining includes gliding along steel lines from one platform to another, often at varied heights and lengths, affording a unique perspective of the countryside below. This sport not only promises an adrenaline rush but also an opportunity to immerse oneself in the heart of Thailand's untamed jungle. Several places across the country offer zip-lining activities, each showing their particular charm.

One of the most popular zip-lining sites in Thailand is Chiang Mai, a city famed for its rich culture and closeness to deep jungles. Here, adventure enthusiasts can soar through the treetops, taking in panoramic views of the beautiful surroundings. The Flight of the Gibbon is a renowned zip-lining company in Chiang Mai that delivers a safe and exhilarating experience, featuring various lines that fly guests through the jungle canopy.

The Island of Koh Phi Phi is yet another remarkable place for zip-lining, this tropical paradise offers a distinct touch to the zip-lining experience. Adventurers can slide from one limestone cliff to another, appreciating the breathtaking coastal panorama and the azure ocean below. The combination of zip-lining and the magnificent island landscape offers an amazing adventure.

In the southern portion of Thailand, near Phuket, the Hanuman World Zipline provides a distinct perspective of the country's natural splendor. With a number of thrilling lines that crisscross through the jungle, tourists may have an adrenaline-pumping adventure while also learning about the local flora and fauna. This instructional part of the event adds a degree of complexity to the adventure, making it both exhilarating and enlightening.

Reputable firms adhere to high safety standards, offering participants with excellent equipment, skilled guides, and extensive safety briefings. This ensures that guests may completely enjoy the experience while reducing any potential risks.

For individuals worried about environmental effects, several zip-lining operations in Thailand prioritize sustainability. They generally engage in eco-friendly methods, such as employing minimum infrastructure to prevent harm to the natural ecosystem. Some even contribute to conservation initiatives and community development, supporting responsible tourism that benefits both visitors and locals.

Cycling and Mountain Biking

Thailand boasts a range of sites suited for cycling and mountain biking, each offering a unique experience. Chiang Mai stands as a premier location, comprising historic temples, scenic valleys, and steep mountain treks. The Mae Hong Son Loop is also a favorite among long-distance riders.

The island of Phuket, on the other hand, caters to people who desire seaside views and tropical surroundings. Riders can visit palm-fringed beaches, and rubber plantations, and even engage in the annual "King of the Mountain" race, an important event in Thailand's cycling calendar.

The diversity of Thailand's geography is reflected in its varied trail selections. For road cyclists, the country has well-maintained roads with mild ascents and descents, making them excellent for leisurely rides. The countryside routes are particularly lovely, letting riders immerse themselves in rural life and experience small markets and villages.

Mountain bikers are spoilt for choice with a selection of trails catering to different ability levels. From the adrenaline-pumping trails of Chiang Mai's Doi Suthep-Pui National Park to the technical demands of Khao Yai National Park, there's something for everyone. Riders can ride through lush jungles, experience waterfalls, and marvel at panoramic vistas as they tackle varied terrains.

Cycling and mountain biking in Thailand offer a unique opportunity to interact with the local culture. Riders will encounter friendly people, see traditional events, and eat authentic cuisine at wayside stalls. Exploring the backroads provides an intimate insight into daily life, where farmers care for their fields and monks collect alms.

To truly appreciate the cultural experience, it's vital to follow local customs and traditions. Dress modestly when visiting temples, and greet residents with the traditional wai gesture. Engaging in cultural sensitivity enhances the journey and develops positive interactions.

Elephant Trekking and Sanctuaries

Among the various attractions the country provides, elephant trekking and sanctuaries stand out as activities that allow visitors to engage intimately with these wonderful creatures. However, new concerns about animal welfare and ethical tourism practices have caused a shift in the way travelers connect with elephants.

Elephant trekking is a traditional activity that involves riding on an elephant as it navigates across diverse terrains, frequently through lush forests and stunning landscapes. Historically, elephants have played a key role in Thailand's culture and economy, functioning as beasts of burden and transportation for millennia. Tourists were lured to elephant trekking owing to the novelty of the experience and the ability to explore the wilderness in a new way.

Over time, awareness has developed regarding the treatment of elephants engaging in trekking activities. Many of these elephants have suffered rigorous training methods and lived in less-than-ideal environments. Reports of physical mistreatment, insufficient living conditions, and overwork have thrown light on the need for better ethical and sustainable methods.

In response to these concerns, elephant sanctuaries have evolved as a more responsible alternative to traditional trekking. These sanctuaries promote the well-being of the elephants, allowing a chance for travelers to watch and interact with these animals in a more natural and humane environment. Unlike regular trekking camps, sanctuaries focus on education and conservation, trying to raise awareness about the issues faced by elephants in captivity.

A visit to an elephant sanctuary often comprises activities like feeding, bathing, and seeing the elephants in their natural habitat. Visitors can learn about the animals' behavior, food, and social dynamics. This hands-on experience builds a stronger relationship with the elephants while supporting their welfare. The emphasis on education helps travelers realize the value of responsible tourism and contributes to the preservation of these amazing creatures.

Tourists seeking to engage with elephants in Thailand should address ethical considerations. Choosing trustworthy sanctuaries that promote the elephants' well-being over entertainment is crucial. Look for places that promote education and environmental efforts rather than commercial activity. Respecting the animals' space and avoiding acts that could cause stress or harm is vital for an ethical interaction.

As the travel business grows, there's an increasing movement toward ethical and sustainable tourism. Many travelers are now opting for experiences that correspond with their values, favoring activities that encourage animal welfare, cultural preservation, and environmental sustainability. Elephant sanctuaries in Thailand exemplify this trend, offering an option for tourists to engage with wildlife in a responsible and humane manner.

Parasailing and Jet Skiing

Parasailing, also referred to as "parascending," combines the exhilaration of flight and the peacefulness of gliding over the ocean. Participants are securely strapped to a colored parachute, which is then hooked to a high-speed motorboat. As the boat accelerates, the parachute lifts the rider into the air, affording stunning panoramic views of the shoreline and the surrounding waterways. The sense of floating effortlessly, with the wind in your hair and the glittering sea underneath you, is a genuinely wonderful experience.

On the other side, jet skiing delivers an amazing journey on the water's surface. A jet ski is a small, powerful watercraft that riders straddle, controlling its speed and direction with handlebars. With the open sea as your playground, you may zoom across the waves, feeling the adrenaline rush as you navigate through the water. The flexibility to explore coves, bays, and hidden beaches at your own pace makes jet skiing a thrilling and dynamic way to discover the beauty of Thailand's coastal locations.

Tourists visiting Thailand can enjoy these activities at several sites across the country, but some of the most popular spots include Phuket, Pattaya, and Koh Samui.

Phuket provides an array of water sports businesses along its lovely beaches. Patong Beach, in particular, is a center for both parasailing and jet skiing. Tourists can order rides directly from sellers on the beach or through their hotels. Additionally, Kata Beach and Karon Beach provide similar possibilities for individuals wanting exhilarating water excursions.

Pattaya, known for its dynamic nightlife and boisterous atmosphere, also offers many options for parasailing and jet skiing. The waters of Pattaya Beach are studded with multicolored parachutes and jet skis. Travelers can indulge in these activities while enjoying the vibrant ambiance of the city.

Koh Samui as described previously, is a picturesque island in the Gulf of Thailand, providing a more calm location for water sports aficionados. Chaweng Beach and Lamai Beach are well-known sites for parasailing and jet skiing. The calmer waters around the island provide a distinct experience compared to the more busy beaches on the mainland.

Before partaking in either of these activities, it's vital for tourists to consider safety. Reputable operators adhere to strict safety requirements, offering participants adequate equipment, instructions on how to control the equipment, and guidelines to follow during the experience. Wearing life jackets and following the directions of skilled professionals helps ensure a secure and pleasurable adventure.

Golfing

Thailand's golf tourist business has been on a steady ascent, thanks to its remarkable choice of courses situated against stunning surroundings. The country's tropical environment allows for year-round golfing, making it an attractive destination for people wishing to escape cooler regions. The combination of wonderful weather and perfectly built golf courses has made Thailand a golfer's dream.

One of the most recognized golfing regions in Thailand is Phuket, it provides a beautiful backdrop for players. Courses like Red Mountain and Blue Canyon Country Club are located amidst beautiful hills, giving not only a test of ability but also breathtaking panoramic views.

Moving north, Chiang Mai enjoys a milder environment and is home to numerous superb courses. The Chiang Mai Highlands Golf and Spa Resort is a highlight, noted for its gorgeous layout amidst mountains and valleys. This region offers a pleasant change of scenery and a chance to discover Thailand's cultural legacy beyond its beaches.

The capital city, Bangkok, is not only a bustling metropolis but also a destination for outstanding golfing. The Thai Country Club and Alpine Golf Club are just two examples of courses that combine world-class play with the convenience of being near the heart of the city. This allows golfers to explore Bangkok's rich history and bustling street life when they're not on the course.

For those seeking an unequaled blend of luxury and golf, Hua Hin meets the bill perfectly. This resort town is filled with high-end hotels and has championship courses like Black Mountain Golf Club. Golfers can indulge in a round of golf while enjoying gorgeous beach vistas and the region's laid-back environment.

What truly makes golfing in Thailand different is the friendliness and hospitality of the local people. From caddies delivering professional assistance to attentive employees assuring a flawless encounter, Thai culture plays a key role in enriching the golfing journey. The ability to eat wonderful Thai cuisine both on and off the course adds a layer of culinary delight to the overall experience.

To cater to golf tourists, Thailand has constructed a solid infrastructure. The country features sophisticated transportation alternatives, making it easy to travel between courses and see diverse places. Additionally, golf tour operators and travel agencies specialize in building personalized golfing vacations that suit every need and choice.

Bungee Jumping and Skydiving

Bungee jumping, a sport that originated from the Pacific islands of Vanuatu, has garnered tremendous appeal worldwide for its sheer boldness and the adrenaline rush it gives. In Thailand, one can indulge in this nerve-wracking experience at various venues, each having its own distinct twist. The most recognized place for bungee jumping is the Jungle Bungy Jump in Phuket. Nestled within beautiful foliage, this facility provides thrill-seekers the option to leap from a tall platform positioned over a lovely lagoon. With a choice of jump techniques available, from basic dives to tandem leaps, participants can customize their experience to match their comfort level.

For those seeking an even more extreme flying encounter, skydiving beckons as the ultimate choice. Skydiving is a heart-pounding activity that allows participants to freefall from an airplane before safely deploying a parachute. Thailand's varied landscape, notably its magnificent coastline and green hinterlands, makes for breathtaking skydiving sites. Among the popular spots is Pattaya, which has spectacular views of the Gulf of Thailand throughout the descent. The experience here is heightened by the juxtaposition of the Turquoise Ocean and expansive metropolitan surroundings. Moreover, the southern province of Chonburi gives an option to tandem jump, allowing even beginners to experience this adrenaline-charged feat under the careful guidance of an expert instructor.

Participating in bungee jumping and skydiving in Thailand is not just about the adrenaline rush; it's also about the overall experience. The build-up, from the anticipation to the actual plunge, is a mental challenge that pushes folks beyond their comfort zones. The spectacular landscapes visible during the activity give an aspect of surreal beauty that contrasts with the heart-pounding exhilaration. The camaraderie among fellow thrill-seekers and the sense of accomplishment after completing the leap contribute to the entire adventure.

While bungee jumping and skydiving are accessible to most, there are important precautions to keep in mind. Participants should be in generally excellent health, free from conditions that may be aggravated by the acute physical sensations. It's also recommended to obey any rules supplied by the operators regarding attire, footwear, and medical constraints.

Conclusion
Thailand's immense natural beauty and diversified landscapes make it a delight for travelers seeking outdoor pursuits. From rock climbing and trekking to diving and animal adventures, the region provides a wide selection of physical activities that cater to all levels of adventurers. Beyond the pleasure of

these activities, travelers also have the opportunity to connect with the local culture, immerse themselves in breathtaking scenery, and create wonderful memories. Whether it's scaling limestone cliffs, riding through historical monuments, or exploring the aquatic world, Thailand definitely has something for any adventurous soul. So, pack your kit, start on a voyage of exploration, and let Thailand's outdoor treasures captivate your heart and spirit.

Dialects and Language

The official language of Thailand is Thai, which is spoken by the majority of the population and serves as a unifying factor across the country. Thai, or "Siamese" as it was originally referred to, has evolved through centuries and is defined by its tonal quality. It incorporates five tones that can vary the meaning of a word, contributing to the intricacy of the language. Thai is written using the Thai script, an attractive writing system with a separate alphabet that consists of 44 consonants and 15 vowels. This script is read from left to right and is usually written without gaps between words.

While Thai is the major language, numerous dialects are spoken in different regions of Thailand. One of the most significant dialects is Isan, spoken in the northeastern region. Isan has close ties to the Lao language and shares characteristics with the Laotian dialect. Due to its physical proximity to Laos, Isan exhibits historical linkages between the two regions.

Moving south, the region around Bangkok and central Thailand is where Standard Thai is most popular due to its significance in government, media, and education. Standard Thai serves as a lingua franca, enabling communication between speakers of diverse regional dialects.

In the north, the Lanna Kingdom's influence is reflected in the Northern Thai dialect, frequently referred to as "Kham Muang." This dialect is defined by its unusual vocabulary and pronunciation, distinguishing it apart from the center dialect. Additionally, the Shan and Tai Yai people in the northern region speak dialects linked to languages spoken in surrounding countries such as Myanmar and China's Yunnan province.

The southern region of Thailand is linguistically varied, with several dialects spoken among distinct ethnic groups. The southern dialects have been impacted by past commerce and cultural interactions with neighboring nations like Malaysia and Indonesia. In the Deep South, the Yawi language, a form of Malay, is spoken by the Malay-Muslim minority.

In recent years, due to increased migration and globalization, languages from various parts of the world have found their way into Thailand's linguistic landscape. English, as a worldwide lingua franca, is widely taught in schools and is used in different businesses, especially in the tourism sector.

Thailand's linguistic variety is not restricted to its native languages. With its thriving tourism economy, the country has become a melting pot of languages from throughout the world. In tourist-centric locations, it's typical to hear languages such as Mandarin, Japanese, Korean, Russian, and more, reflecting the vast array of visitors who travel to the country.

The intertwining of languages and dialects in Thailand can be considered a reflection of the nation's history, culture, and interactions with surrounding countries. The linguistic tapestry that has formed over centuries stands as a tribute to Thailand's willingness to embrace multiple influences while keeping its unique identity.

Conclusion
Thailand's linguistic landscape is a tapestry woven with intricate threads of languages, dialects, and historical influences. From the official language of Thai to regional

dialects like Isan and Northern Thai, each linguistic component gives complexity to the country's cultural mosaic. As Thailand continues to flourish in the modern world, its linguistic diversity remains a monument to its rich legacy and global links.

Weather

Thailand offers a broad selection of experiences to tourists, but, one key component that substantially affects a traveler's adventure is the country's weather. With a tropical climate that varies throughout regions, recognizing Thailand's weather patterns is vital for planning a good vacation.

Thailand's climate can be broadly classified into three seasons: the hot season, the rainy season, and the cold season. These seasons are dictated by the country's geographical location, monsoon winds, and proximity to the equator.

The hot season, which stretches from March through June, is marked by high temperatures and humidity. This period is perfect for beach fans and sunbathers as coastal areas receive clear skies and pleasant waves. However, exploring cities during this season can be hot, forcing many travelers to seek sanctuary in air-conditioned shops or indoor attractions.

The rainy season, running from July to October, is characterized by the southwest monsoon winds, bringing considerable rainfall to most sections of the country. While this season could deter some vacationers, it also has its appeal. The landscapes turn into lush greenery, waterfalls swell to life, and the crowds thin out. The rainfall normally occurs in brief, powerful bursts, leaving pockets of time for outdoor activities. It's advisable to carry rain gear and arrange inside activities as well.

The chilly season, from November through February, is undoubtedly the greatest time to visit Thailand. With cooler temperatures and lesser humidity, it provides a great climate for exploration. This is the main tourist season due to the agreeable weather, making it necessary to reserve lodgings and activities in advance. Northern destinations like Chiang Mai and Chiang Rai endure colder weather, while southern areas like Phuket and Krabi remain warm and pleasant.

Within these broad seasons, Thailand's different areas demonstrate modest variances in weather. Northern Thailand, including cities like Chiang Mai, gets milder temperatures during the cold season and is famed for its vivid festivals and cultural activities. Central Thailand, home to Bangkok, has a similar climate trend to the rest of the country, with probably somewhat milder temperatures. Southern Thailand, containing renowned beach resorts like Phuket, Krabi, and Koh Samui, is impacted by the monsoon winds and sees its rainy season often lasting longer than in other locations.

It's crucial to be aware of the weather conditions during your precise travel dates. While Thailand's climate is largely predictable, unexpected weather phenomena like tropical storms can occur, especially during the transitional periods between seasons. Keeping an eye on weather forecasts and staying current on local news might help you prepare for any potential disruptions to your activities.

Conclusion
Thailand's weather is an important issue to consider when arranging a vacation to this interesting country. Each season has its own set of advantages and challenges, appealing to different types of travelers. Whether you're seeking tropical weather, lush scenery, or a combination of both, understanding Thailand's climate patterns will surely enhance your trip experience. Just remember to prepare appropriately,

be updated about local weather reports, and be flexible with your itinerary to make the most of your trip to the Land of Smiles.

Getting Here

When organizing your relaxing trip to Thailand, you'll need to consider the numerous routes to travel there. From air travel to overland transportation, Thailand offers a multitude of options to fit your preferences and budget.

Air Travel
For most international travelers, flying is the primary and frequently the most convenient means of reaching Thailand. Suvarnabhumi Airport in Bangkok is the country's principal international gateway. Numerous airlines operate flights to Thailand from major cities worldwide. The frequency of flights and the range of carriers available ensure that finding a good alternative for your schedule and budget shouldn't be a difficulty.

Direct Flights: Direct flights are the most straightforward way to visit Thailand. They reduce the stress of layovers and connecting flights, ensuring a smoother trip. Numerous locations, including New York, London, Dubai, Beijing, and Sydney, have direct flights to Bangkok and other important Thai cities.

Connecting Flights: If there aren't any direct flights from your departure city, connecting flights are a wonderful choice. These flights could take a bit longer due to layovers, but they frequently allow greater flexibility in terms of departure dates and times. Connecting flights can allow you to explore an extra place during your journey.

Overland Routes: While air travel is the most frequent means to enter Thailand, overland routes offer a distinct and adventurous experience. If you're an intrepid traveler, consider crossing borders by rail, bus, or even motorcycle.

Train Journeys

Traveling by train to Thailand can be a picturesque and relaxed way to commence your adventure. The train network connects neighboring nations like Malaysia and Cambodia to Thailand. The voyage gives spectacular views of landscapes, the opportunity to interact with locals, and a chance to experience the adventure itself.

Bus Trips

Long-distance buses are an economical choice for reaching Thailand. Bus services connect cities within Southeast Asia, allowing you to tour adjacent countries on your trip to Thailand. This way of travel is suitable for budget-conscious travelers and those who appreciate the excitement of an extended road ride.

Motorcycle Expeditions

For the genuinely daring, embarking on a motorcycle adventure to Thailand is an option worth considering. While this route demands meticulous planning and preparation, it offers an unrivaled sense of freedom and a deeper connection with the places you'll pass.

Cruise and Ferries

If you prefer to arrive by sea, Thailand's coastal cities accept cruise ships and ferries. Phuket and other coastal places have ports that accept international cruise lines. This choice allows you to mix the excitement of a cruise trip with the thrill of visiting Thailand's coastline.

Conclusion

Whether you're drawn to the convenience of air travel, the excitement of overland routes, or the romanticism of coming by sea, Thailand provides a diversity of ways to begin your vacation. Your choice of transportation will depend on your travel style, budget, and the experiences you want to collect along the way. Regardless of how you choose to travel there, your arrival in Thailand is guaranteed to signal the beginning of an incredible trip in a country rich with culture, history, and natural beauty.

Top Attractions

Thailand offers an extraordinary blend of old traditions, modern conveniences, and natural beauty. From the bustling streets of Bangkok to the peaceful beaches of Phuket, Thailand provides a broad choice of tourist attractions that suit any traveler's tastes, below are some popular tourist attractions in Thailand:

Grand Palace, Bangkok

The Grand Palace, located in the center of Bangkok, is a spectacular and recognizable representation of the country's rich history, culture, and royal legacy. Spread across a vast area of 218,400 square meters, the Grand Palace stands as a stunning tribute to Thailand's architectural genius, exquisite design, and aesthetic majesty.

Built in 1782 during the reign of King Rama I, the Grand Palace served as the royal residence of the Thai monarchs for nearly a century. Its awe-inspiring architecture mixes elements of traditional Thai design with inspirations from numerous other civilizations, resulting in a harmonic blend that is both visually attractive and culturally significant. The palace complex has various structures, halls, pavilions, and courtyards, each fulfilling a particular role.

At the center of the Grand Palace rises the Wat Phra Kaew, or the Temple of the Emerald Buddha. This sacred place houses the highly regarded Emerald Buddha statue, masterfully carved from a single block of jade and draped in golden robes that are changed according to the changing seasons by the Thai King. The temple itself is embellished with elaborate features, gilded spires, and colorful mosaic mosaics that exhibit the finest craftsmanship of Thai artists.

The Outer Court of the palace houses various administrative facilities, notably the Amarinda Hall, where important royal ceremonies and parties are place. Visitors are typically in awe of the carefully maintained gardens, gorgeous statues, and extravagant decorations that decorate this region. The Inner Court, on the other hand, is where the king's royal consorts and daughters dwelt. This part of the palace also features the Chakri Maha Prasat Hall, a rare blend of Thai and Western architectural styles that serves as the Grand Palace's primary audience hall.

As tourists explore the Grand Palace complex, they will definitely be charmed by the rich features that adorn the buildings and structures. Elaborate gilded patterns, elaborate stucco sculptures, and intricate frescoes reflect numerous scenes from Thai mythology, literature, and history. The

Palace's design is supposed to replicate the Thai image of heaven, with the center depicting Mount Meru, the mythological home of the gods.

While the Grand Palace has a rich history, it is still very much a living part of Thailand's present. Even now, it continues to be used for numerous formal ceremonies and events, adding to its prominence as a cultural and historical hub.

Visiting the Grand Palace is a fascinating experience that offers guests an immersive trip through Thailand's past, craftsmanship, and spirituality. However, there are crucial considerations for travelers contemplating a visit. Modest clothes are necessary — both men and women should cover their shoulders, arms, and legs. It's best to wear comfortable shoes as there's a large amount of walking involved. Visitors should also be prepared for crowds, as the Grand Palace is a famous tourist site.

Wat Arun, Bangkok

Located on the western bank of the Chao Phraya River in Bangkok, Wat Arun, commonly known as the "Temple of Dawn," stands as an iconic structure that possesses not only architectural grandeur but also historical significance.

Wat Arun's most noticeable feature is its central tower, or prang, which reaches a height of nearly 70 meters, making it one of the highest structures in Bangkok. The prang is ornamented with elaborate mosaics created from shards of Chinese porcelain, reflecting the sunlight in a spectacular display of colors. The tower's climbing stages depict the steps towards enlightenment in Buddhist teachings.

Visitors can tour the temple's four smaller prangs, each dedicated to a different Hindu god. The architecture smoothly integrates parts of Thai and Khmer forms, demonstrating the historical connections between these nations. The highly carved spires are the result of careful craftsmanship, showcasing detailed carvings of mythical creatures, deities, and intricate floral patterns that create a stunning visual spectacle.

Wat Arun's history stretches back to the 17th century when it was originally established by King Taksin as a royal temple. The temple's name, "Temple of Dawn," is attributed to the Hindu god Aruna, signifying the radiating rays of the rising sun. Throughout its history, Wat Arun experienced various repairs and extensions, each contributing to the temple's unique architectural blend.

The center prang, which is the feature of the temple, was constructed later during the reign of King Rama II. The central prang's design is thought to be influenced by Mount Meru, the mythological center of the universe in Buddhist cosmology. Wat Arun has also acted as the background for several royal rituals, illustrating the junction of spirituality and royalty in Thai society.

Tourists visiting Wat Arun might experience a strong sense of awe and wonder as they tour its grounds. The temple complex has various structures, courtyards, and walkways. The steep staircases leading to the central prang offer an exciting ascent and reward panoramic views of the surrounding area. As visitors climb, they'll be charmed by the beautiful embellishments that adorn the temple's walls, demonstrating the passion and expertise of the craftsmen who made them.

The temple's courtyard is filled with statues of legendary creatures and guardian characters, adding to the sense of mystique and mysticism. The tranquil setting fosters quiet reflection, making it a great place to escape the hectic metropolitan surroundings of Bangkok.

Wat Arun is not only a tourist attraction; it remains an active place of worship and a vital element of Thailand's cultural environment. It is a treasured destination for Buddhists, where religious events and rituals take place regularly. Visitors are encouraged to be mindful of the religious practices and cultural significance of the temple while appreciating its beauty.

Wat Pho, Bangkok

Wat Pho, officially known as Wat Phra Chetuphon Vimolmangklararm Rajwaramahaviharn, is a prominent Buddhist temple located in the center of Bangkok. Renowned for its huge size, beautiful architecture, and historical significance, Wat Pho stands as one of Thailand's most recognizable and visited attractions. As a must-see location for tourists, this temple complex offers a rich tapestry of cultural, spiritual, and aesthetic experiences.

Dating back to the 16th century, during the time of King Rama I, Wat Pho was created as a center for scholarship and meditation. The temple's greatest claim to fame is the huge reclining Buddha statue, which measures an astonishing 46 meters (150 feet) in length and 15 meters (49 feet) in height. This golden beauty is not only a religious symbol but also a wonderful achievement of engineering and craftsmanship. Visitors are typically awed by the sheer grandeur and tranquil countenance of the reclining Buddha, whose feet are delicately adorned with mother-of-pearl inlays exhibiting auspicious symbols.

Beyond the renowned statue, Wat Pho contains a huge courtyard that houses several temples, chapels, and stupas. The temple grounds occupy an area of approximately 80,000 square meters, offering travelers a large and comprehensive exploration experience. The complex is created in a traditional Thai architectural style, marked by exquisite detailing, brilliant colors, and extravagant ornamentation.

One of the features of Wat Pho is its status as a center for traditional Thai massage and medicine. The temple is home to the first Thai massage school in the country, where tourists can receive real Thai massage treatments provided by experienced therapists. The therapeutic and comprehensive approach of Thai massage has drawn travelers seeking relaxation and wellness, making Wat Pho a unique destination that integrates spirituality with physical well-being.

The temple's multiple courtyards and gardens provide a tranquil place for contemplation and relaxation. The grounds are ornamented with many statues, murals, and shrines that reflect scenes from Thai mythology, history, and Buddhist teachings. The exquisite artwork and elaborate mosaics offer insights into the country's cultural past, while the quiet ambiance encourages tourists to find moments of tranquility amid the hectic city.

Wat Pho also bears the title of Thailand's first public university. Its historical significance as a center for education is reflected in the temple's emphasis on conserving knowledge and culture. The temple houses a significant collection of inscriptions, relics, and sculptures that provide a thorough picture of Thai history, religion, and art. Exploring the temple's museum allows travelers to delve further into Thailand's past and develop a greater respect for its cultural heritage.

Visiting Wat Pho provides not just a scenic extravaganza but also a spiritual trip. The temple's tranquil ambiance invites guests to experience a moment of relaxation from their busy lives, promoting a sense of connectedness to both the past and the present. As visitors meander around the temple's corridors, they can watch worshippers offering prayers, lighting incense, and presenting offerings to the Buddha, getting insight into the spiritual traditions that underpin Thai society.

Jim Thompson House, Bangkok

This lovely location, named after its American founder, has grown as a revered emblem of Thai heritage, luring travelers from around the world to explore its rich beauty and intriguing history.

The mansion, built of a variety of traditional Thai teakwood constructions, exhibits the incredible vision of Jim Thompson himself. An architect, entrepreneur, and art aficionado, Thompson settled in Thailand after World War II and played a significant role in rebuilding the Thai silk industry. His admiration for the country's culture and workmanship is evident in the way he methodically built and assembled his dwelling. The complex has six finely built teakwood structures, each rich with intricate carvings and ornamented with rare artworks. The layout of the buildings emphasizes the synergy between the natural surroundings and man-made structures, producing a sense of tranquillity that is so typically Thai.

A tour of the Jim Thompson House is a voyage through time, affording tourists a glimpse into both traditional Thai architecture and the life of its colorful founder. The guided tours, conducted in many languages, reveal the complex tapestry of Thompson's life and his significant impact on the nation. From his collection of artifacts and antiques to the enormous array of silk fabrics he acquired, the house provides a vivid depiction of his great eye for aesthetics and his devotion to conserving the spirit of Thailand's cultural past.

One of the most appealing characteristics of the Jim Thompson House is its verdant garden sanctuary. The verdant terrain, filled with tropical plants and tranquil water features, offers a bit of serenity to the hectic urban backdrop of Bangkok. This well-manicured garden displays Thompson's appreciation for nature and his ability to mix it smoothly with the constructed environment. Visitors often find relief here, taking leisurely strolls through the flora and marveling at how Thompson's sense of design extends even to the outdoor settings.

The house not only honors Thompson's unique taste but also works as a storehouse of traditional Thai workmanship. The complex wood carvings, intricate paintings, and magnificent silk tapestries on show are typical of Thailand's cultural past. Visitors are offered an opportunity to admire the sophisticated skills that have been passed down through centuries and to observe how they have been flawlessly merged into the modern context.

However, the Jim Thompson House is not without its mysteries. The inexplicable disappearance of its creator in 1967 has left an everlasting mark on its history. To this day, suspicions and theories surround Thompson's vanishing act, contributing to the aura of mystique that envelops the property. As guests explore the house, they are presented with the lingering question of what transpired on that fatal day, adding an air of suspense to their cultural immersion.

Bangkok Art and Culture Center

The Bangkok Art and Culture Center (BACC) stands as a vivid monument to Thailand's rich artistic heritage and modern cultural landscape. Situated in the midst of the busy metropolis, this historic institution serves both locals and tourists with an immersive experience that captures the nation's artistic journey. Spanning six levels and presenting a broad mix of exhibitions, performances, and seminars, the BACC is a must-visit site for anybody wishing to delve into Thailand's artistic essence.

The BACC's architecture itself is a combination of modernism and history, symbolizing the country's capacity to smoothly blend the ancient with the contemporary. Its clean forms and towering glass panels clash with the surrounding urban surroundings, producing an intriguing visual contrast that attracts visitors. Once inside, the entire essence of Thailand's art and culture unfurls.

Exhibitions at the BACC include a wide spectrum, ranging from traditional Thai art forms to cutting-edge modern works. The center provides a platform for both established artists and rising talents, giving a dynamic area for creativity to develop. Galleries are deliberately arranged to allow visitors to wander through many artistic movements, demonstrating the history of Thai art across time.

Traditional Thai art, profoundly established in the country's cultural history, finds its home within the BACC's walls. Intricately constructed sculptures, intricate paintings, and decorative antiques offer views into Thailand's past, exhibiting the craftsmanship and meaning that distinguish these artistic creations. Visitors may appreciate the subtle dance of faith and artistry, which has been important to Thai society for millennia.

Yet, the BACC is not bound to history; it is a lively center of contemporary art as well. Modern installations challenge standards and push boundaries, enabling spectators to connect with art in new and thought-provoking ways. The center's commitment to promoting innovation has positioned it as a driving force in Thailand's contemporary art scene, attracting artists and fans from across the world.

The BACC is not only a passive viewing environment. It pulsates with activity, holding a plethora of performances, workshops, and events. These encounters enable visitors to connect with art on a personal level, revealing insights into the creative process and the stories behind the pieces. Workshops might span from traditional Thai dance to current photographic techniques, strengthening the cultural interchange between producers and spectators.

A bustling café and a well-stocked bookstore further improve the BACC experience. The café gives a space for reflection and discussion, while the bookstore is a treasure trove of knowledge, including art books, catalogs, and literature that dive into Thailand's cultural tapestry.

Ayutthaya Historical Park

Spanning an area of 289 hectares, this UNESCO World Heritage Site provides tourists with a captivating voyage back in time to the brilliant era of the Ayutthaya Kingdom, which prospered from the 14th to the 18th century. The park, located just north of Bangkok, stands as a tribute to the kingdom's majesty and the indomitable spirit of its people.

The Ayutthaya Historical Park is a huge complex comprising of awe-inspiring ruins, temples, and palaces that once graced the capital city of the Ayutthaya Kingdom. The site's historical significance comes from its role as the second capital of the Siamese Kingdom when it emerged as a major hub of trade, diplomacy, and culture. Today, the park remains a living museum, conserving the architectural marvels that were left in the wake of the kingdom's destruction owing to invasions by surrounding kingdoms.

One of the park's most prominent features is Wat Mahathat, a temple complex noted for the enigmatic Buddha head encased by the roots of a huge banyan tree. This artwork has become a symbol of the site, encapsulating the mix of nature and spirituality that is important to Ayutthaya's heritage. The central prang (tower) of Wat Ratchaburana, another remarkable temple, stands tall as a symbol of the kingdom's religious and architectural strength.

As tourists explore the park, they will meet a myriad of chedis (stupas) and prangs, each distinctively designed and ornamented with elaborate carvings that narrate tales of the past. The calm ambiance, combined with the relics of collapsed constructions, produces an atmosphere of introspection and reverence. The park also features the Royal Palace, showcasing the regal lifestyle of the Ayutthaya royalty through its tall spires and ceremonial rooms.

The Ayutthaya Historical Park is separated into four zones: the Historical Park, the Central Island, the Eastern Island, and the Western Island. Each zone offers a particular view of the kingdom's diverse legacy. The Historical Park contains the central region, housing many of the prominent ruins, while the Central Island hosts Wat Mahathat and Wat Ratchaburana. The Eastern Island features the majestic Wat Na Phra Meru, and the Western Island exhibits the massive Wat Chaiwatthanaram, with its towering prang and riverfront setting.

To make the most of a visit to the Ayutthaya Historical Park, travelers are recommended to embark on guided excursions or rent bicycles to explore the wide expanse. The stories behind each structure come alive through experienced guides, who convey the historical, cultural, and architectural backdrop that influenced the kingdom's past. Biking through the park offers a slow and immersive experience, allowing visitors to marvel at the intricacy of the ruins up close and absorb the tranquil surroundings.

For those looking to delve deeper into the Ayutthaya experience, adjacent museums offer antiques, interactive displays, and historical narratives that complement the outdoor excursion. The Chao Sam Phraya National Museum is a popular pick, featuring a remarkable collection of objects ranging from ceramics to religious sculptures, all of which provide insights into the daily life and artistic triumphs of the Ayutthaya period.

Chiang Mai Old City

Wat Chedi Luang

Nestled in the heart of northern Thailand, the Chiang Mai Old City remains a living witness to the rich history and cultural legacy of the region. This quaint square-shaped enclave is ringed by remnants of a moat and historic city walls, providing travelers with a voyage back in time as they explore its cobblestone alleys, complex temples, and bustling marketplaces. Spanning an area of around 1.5 square kilometers, the Old City is a sanctuary for travelers looking to immerse themselves in a unique blend of history, architecture, and local culture.

The Walls and Moat: The Old City's distinctive feature is the crumbling city walls and a surrounding moat that were built in the 13th century to secure the city from prospective invaders. These architectural marvels not only serve as a tribute to the city's historical significance but also provide a lovely backdrop for visitors to document their Chiang Mai experience. The walls have been painstakingly kept and operate as a physical border between the modernism outside and the cultural sanctuary within.

Temples Galore: Within the limits of the Old City, more than 30 temples, or "wats," await exploration. These halls of worship demonstrate a fascinating blend of Lanna, Thai, and Burmese architectural elements. Among the most recognized is Wat Phra Singh, a masterpiece famed for its beautiful Lanna-style golden facade and the revered Buddha picture it shelters. Another jewel is Wat Chedi Luang, noted for its high pagoda that previously held the Emerald Buddha. Each temple has a tale, encouraging visitors to discover the spiritual and aesthetic journey of the region.

Historical value: Beyond its physical splendor, the Old City possesses historical value as the former capital of the Lanna Kingdom. Its streets murmur tales of old trade routes, royal dynasties, and cultural exchanges. The Three Kings Monument, located near the middle of the Old City, pays honor to the monarchs who played a key part in shaping the city's legacy. Museums and cultural centers, such as the Chiang Mai Historical Center, further unravel the city's past, allowing a greater insight into its evolution.

Local Markets and Cuisine: A trip through the Old City's streets shows a colorful tapestry of local life. The neighborhood is famed for its markets, with the Sunday Walking Street Market being a highlight. This vibrant market spans Ratchadamnoen Road and offers a diversity of handicrafts, textiles, and street cuisine that represent the artistry and flavors of the region. Visitors can relish traditional foods like khao soi, a noodle soup with thick coconut curry, or indulge in vivid fruit drinks and exquisite pastries.

Cultural Exchange and Modern Vibes: While rooted in history, the Chiang Mai Old City also embraces modernity. The combination of centuries-old temples with contemporary art galleries, cafes, and boutique guesthouses produces a unique blend of history and the present. Travelers get the opportunity to meet with local artists, attend seminars, and experience the merging of ancient skills with contemporary inventiveness.

Doi Suthep, Chiang Mai

Wat Phra That Doi Suthep

Doi Suthep, a mesmerizing mountain located near Chiang Mai in Northern Thailand, stands as an important cultural and natural landmark that entices travelers from across the world. This famous place, also referred to as Doi Suthep-Pui National Park, offers a blend of spectacular beauty, religious purity, and historical appeal.

Rising roughly 1,676 meters above sea level, Doi Suthep is famed for its magnificent temple, Wat Phra That Doi Suthep, sitting majestically on its peak. To fully appreciate the vista, one goes on a climb up the mountain, navigating a winding route that leads to the temple. Adventurous souls might opt for a climb up the Naga Staircase, an outstanding staircase covered with mythical snake sculptures, numbering over 300 steps, which adds an aura of mysticism to the trip.

Upon reaching the temple, tourists are met by a magnificent golden chedi, or pagoda, which enshrines holy relics. The chedi's exquisite design symbolizes a blend of Lanna and Theravada Buddhist creativity. Surrounding the chedi, visitors are exposed to panoramic views of Chiang Mai and the beautiful surroundings below, giving a calm atmosphere for silent contemplation and meditation.

Doi Suthep's spiritual importance extends back millennia. According to mythology, a relic purported to be from the Buddha was mounted on the back of a white elephant, which then climbed the mountain and circled until finding its resting place, designating the site for the construction of the temple. This history provides an air of reverence for the temple, making it a pilgrimage spot for committed Buddhists and a place of spiritual awakening for those seeking peace.

Beyond its religious importance, Doi Suthep also offers ample chances for nature aficionados and adventure seekers. The national park surrounding the temple boasts various flora and fauna, with established pathways for hiking, allowing tourists to immerse themselves in the cold mountain air and lush tropical surroundings. During the trek, the sights of waterfalls, wild orchids, and numerous bird species add to the park's attractiveness.

For a well-rounded experience, it's advised to explore the adjacent Hmong Hill Tribe Village, where visitors can witness traditional Hmong culture and craftsmanship. Here, bustling marketplaces feature complex textiles, handmade crafts, and local cuisines, allowing an opportunity to support the local community and take home unique keepsakes.

When arranging a visit to Doi Suthep, it's crucial to consider the weather. The milder and drier months between November and February are often regarded as the optimum time to explore the area. However, even during the rainy season from June to October, the mist-shrouded mountains and occasional rain showers can give a romantic and mysterious touch to the experience.

Pai

Nestled amid the beautiful mountains of Northern Thailand as well, Pai is a charming and scenic town that has gained a reputation as a tranquil hideaway for those wanting a break from the rush and bustle of city life.

Located around 135 kilometers northwest of Chiang Mai, the travel to Pai is an adventure in itself. The meandering roads leading to the town offer spectacular views of the surrounding mountains and valleys, making travel an integral part of the experience. Many travelers choose motorbike rentals to navigate the twists and turns, adding an element of excitement to their adventure.

Pai's natural sceneries are a big appeal for travelers. The hamlet is surrounded by beautiful forests, rolling hills, and magnificent waterfalls. Mo Paeng Waterfall, for instance, is a favored destination for travelers who wish to cool off in its natural pools after a short climb. The Pai Canyon, with its tiny ridges and panoramic views, is another must-visit site for hikers and photographers alike.

One of Pai's most unique attractions is its bustling cultural scene. The village attracts a diverse audience of Thai and international artists, musicians, and authors, giving rise to a flourishing arts and crafts culture. Walking through the streets, visitors will find several galleries, boutique shops, and street markets where they may purchase locally made handicrafts, paintings, and clothing. The Pai Walking Street, which comes alive every night with food stalls and entertainment, is a hub for sampling wonderful street cuisine and enjoying live music.

A vacation to Pai wouldn't be complete without investigating its spiritual side. The town is home to several gorgeous temples that showcase its blend of civilizations. Wat Phra That Mae Yen, positioned atop a hill, gives amazing panoramic views of Pai and its surroundings. Visitors can ascend the steep stairs to reach the temple and observe the magnificence of the white Buddha statue that stands tall and tranquil.

Pai's quiet and meditative ambiance has also drawn wellness enthusiasts and yoga practitioners from throughout the world. The area boasts various yoga and meditation centers where travelers can revitalize their mind, body, and spirit. The natural surroundings provide the perfect backdrop for practicing mindfulness and attaining inner serenity.

In recent years, Pai has seen an influx of tourists seeking an alternative to Thailand's more crowded locations. Despite its expanding popularity, the town has managed to keep its calm air and escape the trappings of over-commercialization. The slow-paced lifestyle and friendly welcome of the local population make it simple for tourists to feel at home.

Accommodation options in Pai range from inexpensive guesthouses to luxurious boutique resorts. Many of these lodgings integrate harmoniously with the natural surroundings, offering visitors a unique and immersive experience. Some even provide private bungalows overlooking rice terraces or situated within the hills, allowing tourists to wake up to the peaceful sounds of nature.

Phang Nga Bay

Nestled along the southern coast of Thailand, Phang Nga Bay stands as a testament to the awe-inspiring beauty that the natural world can generate. With its labyrinth of limestone karsts, emerald waters, and isolated caverns, the bay has earned its status as a must-visit location for travelers seeking a unique and captivating experience.

Stretching over 400 square kilometers, Phang Nga Bay presents a unique environment that feels almost unearthly. Its most prominent characteristic is the towering limestone karsts that rise sharply from the water's surface. These karsts, built over millions of years by the slow process of erosion, provide a stunning panorama of spires, caves, and hidden lagoons. The contrast between the green flora clinging to these ancient rock formations and the turquoise waters of the bay is definitely a sight to behold.

One of the most popular activities in Phang Nga Bay is exploring its sea caverns, commonly known as "hongs." These subterranean caverns are accessible by kayak during low tide and show a beautiful world inside. Paddling through tight tunnels, visitors are transported to serene, secluded lagoons covered by high cliffs and luxuriant foliage. The hongs provide a unique opportunity to explore the bay's environment up close, as they serve as a sanctuary for varied flora and wildlife, including bats, monkeys, and unusual plants.

James Bond Island, made famous by the 1974 film "The Man with the Golden Gun," is another gem of Phang Nga Bay. Its official name is Koh Tapu, and it's a lone limestone karst that juts abruptly out of the water, flanked by smaller islets. The island's remarkable shape has made it an iconic symbol of the bay, drawing tourists from around the world to marvel at its unusual form and cinematic past.

For those seeking an adventure that mixes pleasure with exploration, kayaking in Phang Nga Bay is a memorable experience. Paddling over the calm waters, tourists can plunge into the bay's complicated network of canals, weaving between the spectacular karsts and soaking in the tranquillity of the surroundings. Many tour providers offer guided kayaking experiences, ensuring that even people with minimum experience may enjoy the beauty of the bay.

Beyond its breathtaking vistas, Phang Nga Bay is also home to a rich and diverse marine ecosystem. Snorkeling and diving aficionados will find themselves in a vivid underwater world, with coral reefs alive with colorful marine life. From vivid fish to fascinating aquatic animals, the bay's underwater realm is a treasure trove waiting to be explored.

To fully engage in the cultural experience of the region, travelers might visit the neighboring floating Muslim town of Koh Panyee. Perched atop stilts over the sea, the settlement offers a look into the traditional way of life of the residents. Visitors can browse through the tiny passageways, see the mosque, and savor fresh seafood dishes in the village's restaurants.

Sukhothai Historical Park

This UNESCO World Heritage Site, spanning an area of approximately 70 square kilometers, is a glimpse into the golden age of Thai civilization that flourished during the 13th and 15th centuries.

The park is organized into five primary zones, each reflecting various architectural and artistic styles that distinguished the Sukhothai era. The core zone, known as the Historic Town, is the focal point of the park, featuring some of the most prominent landmarks. The Great Stupa, with its lotus-bud-shaped dome and elaborate stucco patterns, remains a symbol of Buddhist devotion. Adjacent to it sits the Royal Palace, previously the house of the monarch, encircled by defensive walls and ponds that demonstrate the strategic urban design of the time.

As visitors explore the park, the Ramkhamhaeng National Museum, situated just beyond the main entrance, provides vital context. Exhibits within the museum showcase relics, sculptures, and inscriptions that offer light on the daily lives, beliefs, and achievements of the Sukhothai people. This preparation increases the experience within the park by strengthening one's awareness of the historical significance of the structures.

Moving outside the center zone, the North Zone is a treasure trove of temple complexes. The Wat Phra Pai Luang complex boasts a huge standing Buddha, its placid look creating a sense of tranquility. The Sukhothai Kingdom's commitment to religious devotion is obvious in these temples, distinguished by exquisite stone carvings, graceful stupas, and ornate columns that serve as testaments to the aesthetic quality of the era.

In the West Zone, the Si Satchanalai Historical Park is an addition that offers a quieter and equally exciting experience. The majestic Wat Chang Lom and Wat Chedi Chet Thaeo temples retain the history of exquisite architecture and historical significance. The natural splendor of the park's surroundings provides a tranquil setting for contemplation and exploration.

The Central, North, and West Zones jointly constitute the core of the Sukhothai Kingdom's influence. However, the lesser-explored zones of the East and South reveal hidden gems that complete the mosaic of Sukhothai's legacy. The East Zone is home to Wat Chedi Si Hong, famed for its unique square chedi design, while the South Zone's Wat Chetuphon has a rare reclining Buddha statue, evoking the peacefulness of enlightenment.

To truly enjoy the Sukhothai Historical Park, visitors are suggested to explore either by foot, bicycle, or electric tram. The peaceful roads, rich vegetation, and serene ponds create a serene ambiance, transporting guests to a bygone period. Engaging with educated local guides can provide greater insights into the historical and cultural aspects of the site.

Kanchanaburi

River Kwai Bridge

Nestled in the western portion of Thailand, one of the biggest charms of Kanchanaburi is definitely its spectacular natural scenery. The province is home to rich woods, spectacular mountains, and peaceful rivers, all of which provide enough chances for adventure enthusiasts. The Erawan National Park is a prime example, offering a succession of cascading waterfalls that tempt visitors to stroll along the jungle-clad trails. The crystal-clear ponds at each level of the waterfall are great for a relaxing plunge, allowing guests to connect with nature in a unique way.

However, Kanchanaburi's historical significance is as captivating. The most famous site here is the Bridge on the River Kwai, a heartbreaking reminder of World War II. The bridge is part of the Death Railway, erected by prisoners of war under difficult conditions. The JEATH War Museum nearby provides insight into the lives of individuals who were involved in its construction. Visitors can pay their respects at the Kanchanaburi War Cemetery, where thousands of Allied soldiers were put to rest.

For a more thorough historical experience, the Hellfire Pass Memorial Museum is a touching memorial to the POWs who lost their lives during the railway's construction. The museum's interactive displays and guided tours offer a sobering view into the challenges encountered by people who were part of this awful chapter in history.

Cultural inquiry is another part of Kanchanaburi's attraction. The Wat Tham Sua, or Tiger Cave Temple, is a venerated Buddhist monument built atop a hill, affording panoramic views of the surrounding landscape. Visitors can climb the steep stairway to reach the temple complex, where elaborate statuary and calm meditation rooms await.

To delve deeper into local life, a visit to the Tha Kilen Train Market is recommended. This busy market is built up beside an active railway track, and as the train approaches, traders swiftly fold up their stalls to make space for it. Once the train passes, the market comes alive again with colorful produce, delectable street food, and handicrafts.

Beyond its historical and cultural charms, Kanchanaburi offers a choice of activities for relaxation and rejuvenation. Sai Yok National Park is a tranquil refuge, famed for its hot springs and waterfalls. Travelers can unwind in the natural pools and bathe in the therapeutic advantages of the mineral-rich waters.

Accommodation choices in Kanchanaburi cater to diverse preferences. From riverfront resorts that provide breathtaking views of the Kwai River to quiet boutique guesthouses situated within the town, there's something for every type of traveler.

Ko Samui

Wat Phra Yai

Located in the Gulf of Thailand, Ko Samui is the largest island in the Chumphon Archipelago, recognized for its diverse topography that runs from pristine beaches to lush woods and steep mountains. The island features a tropical environment, typified by a hot season from February to April and a rainy season from September to November. The chilly, dry season from December to January is a popular time for travelers, with temperatures ranging around a moderate 25-28°C (77-82°F).

Beaches and Water Activities
The island's shoreline is lined with postcard-perfect beaches, each offering a unique experience. Chaweng Beach is the most famous, boasting pure white sand and a bustling environment. Lamai Beach, with its easygoing attitude, is a favorite among families. Bophut Beach is recognized for its picturesque Fisherman's Village, offering an insight into the

island's history as a fishing town. Visitors can participate in a wealth of aquatic sports, including snorkeling, scuba diving, kayaking, and even paddleboarding.

Cultural Attractions

Beyond its natural beauty, Ko Samui has a rich cultural heritage. Wat Phra Yai, known as the Big Buddha Temple, contains a huge golden statue visible from kilometers away. Wat Plai Laem is another notable temple, revered for its exquisite architecture and beautiful figure of the goddess Guanyin. The Secret Buddha Garden, buried up in the hills, is a hidden gem boasting a collection of statues and lovely landscapes.

Nightlife and Entertainment

As the sun sets, Ko Samui transforms into a lively nightlife hub. The island offers a variety of entertainment alternatives, from seaside bars and nightclubs to cultural concerts and fire-dancing performances. The Ark Bar Beach Club in Chaweng is famed for its frenetic events, while Fisherman's Village has a popular night market every Friday, featuring shopping, food, and live music.

Luxury Resorts and Wellness Retreats

Koh Samui offers a wide range of guests, including those seeking luxury and relaxation. The island is home to an array of high-end resorts and wellness retreats that offer world-class amenities such as private villas, spa treatments, and gourmet cuisine. Many of these resorts are set in quiet areas, ensuring tranquility and seclusion for guests.

Exploration and Day Trips

While Koh Samui itself is a treasure trove of attractions, it also serves as a gateway to other islands. Many travelers embark on day tours to discover the magnificent Angthong Marine Park, an archipelago of 42 islands noted for its limestone cliffs, hidden lagoons, and colorful marine life. Another popular resort is Ko Pha-ngan, noted for its Full Moon Party and quiet beaches.

Similan Islands

The Similan Islands as described previously, situated in the turquoise seas of the Andaman Sea, are a gorgeous archipelago comprising nine stunning islands. Located off the western coast of Thailand, near the province of Phang Nga, these islands have established a reputation as one of the world's top diving and snorkeling destinations, attracting nature enthusiasts and adventurers from all corners of the globe to Similan Island.

Known for their pristine beauty and abundant marine life, the Similan Islands have been classified as a national park, offering them a level of protection to conserve their natural magnificence. Each island is distinctive in its own right, offering a broad choice of activities for travelers wishing to immerse themselves in the beauties of the sea and the land.

The underwater habitat surrounding the Similan Islands is a delight for divers and snorkelers. Crystal-clear waters, vivid coral reefs, and an astonishing assortment of marine life make this place a must-visit for those who are passionate about exploring the depths of the ocean. The islands are home to an astounding array of fish species, including colorful clownfish, beautiful manta rays, and the majestic whale sharks. The diving locations, with intriguing names such as Elephant Head Rock and East of Eden, give opportunities to view the awe-inspiring grandeur of underwater ecosystems in their full splendor.

Above the waterline, the Similan Islands continue to attract visitors with their natural splendor. Pristine white sandy beaches spread along the shoreline, encouraging guests to relax, soak up the sun, and enjoy the calm surroundings. Hiking trails snake through thick woodlands, offering magnificent overlooks that give sweeping vistas of the surrounding seas and islands.

While the islands are a dream for water sports lovers, they are also a shelter for people who seek a closer connection to nature. The islands are inhabited by rich wildlife, including endemic species such as flying foxes and banded sea snakes. Keen birdwatchers can catch glimpses of several bird species, including Nicobar pigeons and pied imperial pigeons, as they dart through the trees.

Visiting the Similan Islands needs considerable planning. The park is normally open to tourists from November to April, as the weather during this period is more suited to exploration and water activities. Accommodations on the islands are limited and tend to be rustic in style, with bungalows accessible for overnight stays. It's vital to make reservations well in advance to reserve your position and enjoy an uninterrupted island experience.

As an ecologically vulnerable area, appropriate tourism practices are vital when visiting the Similan Islands. Visitors are asked to observe instructions set by the park officials, such as refraining from touching or destroying coral reefs, avoiding feeding or disturbing wildlife, and disposing of garbage correctly to reduce the environmental impact.

Wat Rong Khun (White Temple), Chiang Rai

Wat Rong Khun, popularly known as the White Temple, is a gorgeous and distinctive contemporary Buddhist temple located in Chiang Rai. It distinguishes out for its magnificent architecture, rich detailing, and unique design.

Conceived by renowned Thai artist Chalermchai Kositpipat, Wat Rong Khun is an artistic masterwork that challenges the standards of temple design. Unlike many conventional temples, which have gathered layers of history and architecture over decades, the White Temple was conceptualized and completed in the late 20th and early 21st centuries. This offers it a fresh and distinctive appearance that captivates tourists from around the world.

The temple's name, "Wat Rong Khun," translates to "White Temple" in English, and it is properly titled for its remarkable all-white aspect. The facade of the temple is covered with ornate sculptures and mirrored glass mosaics that dazzle in the sunlight, creating a bizarre and otherworldly environment. The sparkling white color symbolizes purity and the route to enlightenment in Buddhism, enabling guests to go on a spiritual journey as they tour the temple's surroundings.

As visitors approach the main building, they cross a bridge across a small lake that signifies the journey from the cycle of death and rebirth to the state of enlightenment. The bridge is bordered by outreaching hands symbolizing yearning, and creepy sculptures that create thoughts of contemplation and self-awareness.

The main ubosot (ordination hall) is a captivating blend of traditional Thai architecture and contemporary art. The beautiful woodwork and delicate carvings on the exterior are perfectly crafted, displaying Chalermchai's attention to craftsmanship. Inside the hall, though, surprises await. Murals portray a mix of ancient Buddhist themes and modern cultural allusions, including imagery from popular movies, cartoons, and legendary people like Superman and Michael Jackson. These murals offer an insightful perspective on the junction between spirituality and popular culture.

While the exterior and main hall are prominent attractions, Wat Rong Khun is a huge complex that comprises numerous structures and features of appeal. Visitors can visit art galleries, meditation rooms, and smaller shrines. The temple's unique design also extends to its lavatories, which are housed in metallic, futuristic constructions that stand in stark contrast to regular restroom facilities.

The continual construction and expansion of Wat Rong Khun make it an evolving marvel. Chalermchai Kositpipat regards the temple as a lifelong endeavor, and its evolution over time has attracted the interest of both tourists and art fans. Visitors not only observe the creativity of the artist but also the constant progression of his perspective.

Ko Phi Phi Leh

Maya Bay

Nestled in the cerulean waters of the Andaman Sea as well, Ko Phi Phi Leh is a gem of an island located in the southern region of Thailand. With its beautiful beaches, crystal-clear waters, and spectacular limestone cliffs, Ko Phi Phi Leh has acquired global recognition as one of the most stunning and sought-after tourist destinations.

Ko Phi Phi Leh boasts outstanding natural beauty, highlighted by its white sandy beaches and towering limestone structures. One of the island's most renowned sites is Maya Bay, famously portrayed in the movie "The Beach." Enclosed by steep cliffs, Maya Bay's calm waters and diverse marine life make it a snorkeler's paradise. However, it's vital to remember that owing to over-tourism, Maya Bay has been temporarily closed to allow its environment to recover.

Beneath the surface, Ko Phi Phi Leh's aquatic ecology is similarly stunning. With bright coral reefs and a rich assortment of aquatic animals, the island provides outstanding diving and snorkeling opportunities. Sites like Shark Point and Bida Nok are famed for encounters with leopard sharks, blacktip reef sharks, and a diversity of colorful fish. Divers and snorkelers alike will find themselves immersed in an underwater wonderland.

Exploring Ko Phi Phi Leh's coastline offers hidden gems like Loh Samah Bay. Its tranquil seas and magnificent coral formations are great for kayaking or simply observing the environment. Viking Cave, called by its ancient wall murals resembling Viking ships, is another remarkable attraction. It has historical significance as a source of swiftlet nests, which are used in the making of bird's nest soup.

In recent years, concerns about environmental degradation have driven intensified attempts to conserve the island's unique ecosystems. Limiting visitor access to specific locations, like Maya Bay, is part of a bigger endeavor to find a balance between tourism and conservation. Travelers are asked to adhere to responsible tourism practices, such as refraining from touching or damaging coral reefs, correctly disposing of waste, and respecting local wildlife.

Reaching Ko Phi Phi Leh normally takes a ferry voyage from Phuket or Krabi. The island itself does not have hotels due to its protected status, however nearby sister island Ko Phi Phi Don offers a choice of accommodation options. From budget-friendly guesthouses to luxury resorts, tourists can discover lodgings that suit their interests and budgets. Many of these facilities provide planned tours to Ko Phi Phi Leh, offering a flawless exploration experience.

The optimal time to visit Ko Phi Phi Leh is during the dry season, which extends from November to April. The weather is characterized by clear skies, calm seas, and pleasant temperatures. However, this period also corresponds to the main tourist season, so travelers can anticipate bigger crowds and higher rates. The rainy season, from May to October, brings rain and strong seas, making access to the island more problematic.

As the day draws to a close, tourists can revel in Ko Phi Phi Leh's spectacular sunsets. The island's vantage spots, such as the viewpoint above Tonsai Bay on Ko Phi Phi Don, provide the perfect background for an awe-inspiring sunset experience. For those seeking nightlife, Ko Phi Phi Don offers a dynamic atmosphere with beachfront bars, fire displays, and social gatherings that create unforgettable experiences.

Ao Nang

Ao Nang Beach

Ao Nang is a scenic and mesmerizing tourist spot located in the Krabi Province of Thailand. With its spectacular natural beauty, plentiful recreational activities, and energetic atmosphere, Ao Nang has become a preferred destination for vacationers seeking a tropical paradise experience.

Nestled along the Andaman Sea as well, Ao Nang provides stunning views that mix towering limestone cliffs, immaculate white sandy beaches, and crystal-clear turquoise waters. This unique combination produces a captivating setting that is excellent for relaxation and exploration equally. The main beach of Ao Nang offers a postcard-perfect picture, inviting visitors to recline on its sands while soaking in the gorgeous environment.

101

The town of Ao Nang itself is a dynamic hub that offers a combination of local culture and international comforts. The lively streets are lined with a variety of restaurants, pubs, stores, and hotels that cater to every budget. Visitors can enjoy traditional Thai cuisine as well as other delicacies, making it a gastronomic haven for food connoisseurs.

One of the most prominent attractions of Ao Nang is the Four Islands Tour. This expedition takes guests to the lovely islands of Phra Nang, Tup, Chicken, and Poda. Each island possesses its own unique beauty, from the spectacular Phra Nang Cave Beach with its towering limestone cliffs to the quiet Tup Island, accessible by walking during low tide. The Chicken and Poda Islands are renowned for their clean beaches and outstanding snorkeling opportunities, allowing an opportunity to explore the diverse aquatic life of the region.

For adventure seekers, Ao Nang is a fantastic location for exploring the adjacent Railay Beach. Accessible only by boat due to its encirclement by limestone cliffs, Railay is a rock climber's dream, with various climbing routes catering to climbers of all levels. The viewpoint on Railay offers a panoramic panorama that rewards those who undertake the hike with beautiful views of the surrounding area.

The aquatic activities in Ao Nang are another key appeal for tourists. The seas are rich with colorful marine life, making it a superb place for snorkeling and scuba diving. Local tour providers offer a number of opportunities for both beginners and expert divers to explore the underwater world of the Andaman Sea.

Away from the beach, Ao Nang also offers a flavor of native culture and spirituality. The Wat Tham Sua, or Tiger Cave

Temple, is a notable Buddhist temple complex located just a short drive from Ao Nang. It takes its name from a tiger paw print-shaped stone in the cave, and the site provides a hard stair climb to a viewpoint that rewards hikers with a panoramic view of the area.

Golden Triangle

The Golden Triangle, tucked in the northernmost portion of Thailand, comprises the intersection of Thailand, Myanmar, and Laos, this area has been dubbed the "Golden Triangle" due to its past as a significant center for opium cultivation and trade. Presently, the region has changed into a sought-after tourist attraction, offering guests a fantastic experience.

One of the most attractive characteristics of the Golden Triangle is its breathtaking natural setting. With the Mekong River coursing through the center of the province, tourists are treated to stunning landscapes of lush flora, peaceful canals, and rolling hills. The confluence of these three countries produces a unique atmosphere where travelers can stand on the coastlines of one country and gaze across the ocean to two others, a truly amazing sight that represents the essence of the Golden Triangle.

The Golden Triangle is also deep in cultural legacy. It's home to many ethnic communities, each with its own distinct customs and ways of life. Visitors get the opportunity to connect with local communities, learn about their customs, and even participate in workshops to create traditional crafts or enjoy local cuisine. Hill tribes like the Akha, Yao, and Karen give an aspect of authenticity to the encounter, offering insights into their ancient rituals and beliefs. This cultural tapestry provides a deep and profound connection for travelers wishing to understand the human side of the Golden Triangle.

Historically, the Golden Triangle was infamous for its opium trafficking, which flourished in the mid-20th century. The region's strategic location made it a crucial center for the cultivation, production, and smuggling of opium. While the opium trade has declined, vestiges of this dark history can still be examined through museums and exhibits that provide insight into the challenges faced by local communities and the efforts to tackle drug-related concerns. Understanding this historical context adds layers of complexity to the region's identity and serves as a reminder of the tenacity of its people.

For travelers seeking adventure, the Golden Triangle doesn't disappoint. Trekking through the difficult terrain, finding secret towns, and embarking on river cruises down the Mekong River are just a few of the thrilling activities available. The region's unique flora and fauna make it a hub for eco-tourism, drawing nature enthusiasts and wildlife photographers. Trekking paths transport visitors through inaccessible places, exhibiting the natural beauty of the landscape and affording glimpses of indigenous fauna.

Accommodation options in the Golden Triangle range from luxury resorts to boutique lodges that provide beautiful panoramic views. Many of these motels are built to integrate with the landscape and give a comfortable location for guests to relax after a day of sightseeing.

Ko Chang

Nestled in the Gulf of Thailand, the third-largest island in Thailand, Ko Chang offers a total retreat from the frenetic city life. Reaching Koh Chang is an adventure in itself. Accessible by ferry or speedboat, the voyage from the mainland to the island sets the tone for what's to follow. The first glance of the island's undulating geography covered in deep tropical rainforests is enough to evoke a sense of curiosity and awe. The island is famed for its teeming wildlife, and hiking through the lush jungles is a fantastic opportunity to immerse oneself in its natural splendor. Trails such as the one leading to the Klong Plu Waterfall or the Salak Phet Mangrove Walkway allow a chance to view rare flora and animals up close.

Of course, Ko Chang's biggest lure is its magnificent coastline. White sandy beaches and crystal-clear waters stretch along the western side of the island, giving several areas for leisure and water-based sports. White Sand Beach,

Lonely Beach, and Klong Kloi Beach are just a few of the beachside havens where visitors may soak up the sun, enjoy a refreshing swim, or engage in various water activities like snorkeling, kayaking, and diving. The abundant marine life and brilliant coral reefs just offshore make it a paradise for underwater explorers.

For those seeking a bit of adventure, the island doesn't disappoint. Jungle trekking, elephant trekking, and zip-lining are some of the activities that cater to adrenaline enthusiasts. Exploring the island on two wheels is also a popular alternative, with scooter rentals available to travel at your own speed.

Cultural discovery is another part of the Ko Chang experience. The island's tiny fishing communities provide an authentic peek into the lives of the island's residents. Walking around these villages and mingling with inhabitants provides travelers an opportunity to appreciate the traditional way of life that still prevails amidst the rising tourism business.

Culinary adventures are a highlight too. Ko Chang's dining scene offers a blend of international and local flavors. Freshly caught fish is a staple, and coastal eateries serve up scrumptious dishes that satisfy even the most sophisticated palate. Exploring the local night markets is a terrific chance to try authentic Thai street food and immerse oneself in the island's culinary culture.

Accommodation options on Ko Chang cater to a variety of preferences. From budget-friendly guesthouses to magnificent seaside resorts, tourists can choose a place that matches their needs. Waking up to the sound of waves crashing and a view of the ocean is an experience that sticks in the memory long after the vacation has ended.

Ancient Siam (Muang Boran), Samut Prakan

Sanphet Maha Prasat Throne Hall

Ancient Siam, also known as Muang Boran, is a unique open-air museum located in Samut Prakan, encompassing a massive area of 320 acres, Ancient Siam is generally regarded as the world's largest outdoor museum and an epitome of Thai tradition.

Going into Ancient Siam is comparable to going back in time, as the museum painstakingly recreates over a hundred of Thailand's most renowned landmarks, monuments, and constructions from various periods of its history. The exquisite attention to detail and authenticity is awe-inspiring, allowing visitors to see the progression of Thai architecture and culture through the ages.

The museum is organized into numerous sections, each reflecting different locations and times in Thailand. Visitors can visit reproductions of old temples, palaces, traditional residences, and even sacred locations. This diversity offers a complete view of Thailand's architectural progress, from the Ayutthaya period to the Rattanakosin era and beyond. The structures are beautifully made, with complex designs, carvings, and embellishments that pay homage to the artistry of the past.

One of the primary characteristics of Ancient Siam is its accuracy in reflecting the numerous architectural styles and regional influences that have influenced Thailand's past. The attention to detail extends to the surrounding landscapes, which typically replicate the original surroundings of these structures. As visitors travel around the museum's corridors, they are transported to numerous time periods and regions, getting insights into the historical background that shaped each architectural masterpiece.

The museum is not just about the structures; it's also about the cultural value they carry. Visitors can observe traditional performances, ceremonies, and rituals that are a vital aspect of Thai culture. This immersive experience provides a deeper knowledge of the values, beliefs, and traditions that have been passed down through generations.

Beyond architecture and culture, Ancient Siam also has an outstanding collection of antiques and art items that further deepen the visitor's understanding of Thailand's past. Sculptures, paintings, and other artifacts offer a look into the daily lives, habits, and beliefs of the Thai people from different centuries.

Ancient Siam serves as both a tourist attraction and an educational resource. It's a site where tourists can learn about Thailand's history and culture in an entertaining and interactive manner. Schools often organize tours to the museum to provide pupils with a hands-on experience of the country's legacy, building a deeper understanding of their roots.

Khon Kaen

The city is steeped in history and culture, visible in its temples and monuments. The Wat Nong Wang temple is a remarkable landmark, including a tall nine-story stupa that offers panoramic views of the city. Visitors can marvel at the beautiful murals and architectural features while immersing themselves in the spiritual environment.

For an immersion into local heritage, the Khon Kaen National Museum is a must-visit. It houses a remarkable collection of artifacts that trace the region's history, from prehistoric times to the current period. The museum provides unique insights into the traditional way of life of the people in the northeastern Isaan region.

Khon Kaen boasts vibrant markets where visitors can experience the native way of life. The Ton Tann Night Market is a buzzing center of activity, offering a vast choice of street food, handicrafts, and apparel. It's the best place to find souvenirs and immerse oneself in the vivid ambiance of the city after dark.

Nature enthusiasts will find refuge in Khon Kaen's natural beauties. Bueng Kaen Nakhon, a scenic lake in the heart of the city, is a favorite area for leisure and pleasure. Visitors can rent bicycles and pedal along the gorgeous routes or take a boat excursion to fully appreciate the tranquillity of the surroundings.

For those wishing to explore beyond the city limits, Phu Wiang National Park offers a unique experience. Famed for its dinosaur fossils and footprints, the park provides a peek into prehistoric times. The Dinosaur Museum within the park informs visitors about the ancient dinosaurs that previously roamed the region, making it a fascinating stop for both adults and children.

Khon Kaen organizes many events throughout the year that showcase the region's culture and traditions. The Silk Festival exhibits the delicate craft of silk weaving, which is a vital element of the local economy. During this event, guests can observe traditional performances, discover silk production methods, and purchase fine silk products.

Khon Kaen offers a selection of hotel options to meet every budget and inclination. From luxurious hotels to quaint guesthouses, tourists can find a pleasant place to stay while visiting the city and its surroundings. The kindness and hospitality of the residents add to a great experience, making guests feel welcome and at home.

Chiang Rai Night Bazaar

Nestled in the picturesque city of Chiang Rai, the Chiang Rai Night Bazaar serves as a tribute to the complex tapestry of culture and commerce that defines the region. As the sun drops below the horizon and the stars begin to glimmer, the bazaar comes alive, bringing tourists a dazzling blend of local goods, scrumptious cuisine, and exciting entertainment. Spanning over 600 meters along Phaholyothin Road, this lively market is a must-visit location for travelers wanting an immersive Thai experience.

At the heart of the Chiang Rai Night Bazaar sits the vibrant bazaar, where an array of vendors beckons visitors with a kaleidoscope of wares. From delicate handcrafted fabrics and fine silver jewelry to traditional wood carvings and magnificent ceramics, the market gives an opportunity to indulge in Thailand's cultural history. Many of these products are produced by skilled artisans from the neighboring villages, allowing a genuine peek into the local workmanship that has been passed down through generations.

The culinary delights of the Night Bazaar are equally intriguing. The perfume of sizzling skewers and delicious curries wafts through the air, luring pedestrians to sample the local cuisine. From delectable Pad Thai, the renowned stir-fried noodle dish, to the flavorful Som Tum, a spicy papaya salad, the bazaar's food stalls are a culinary journey waiting to be explored. Adventurous cuisine fans can relish strange meals like fried insects, a unique and adventurous delight that epitomizes the region's robust gastronomic offerings.

Beyond the shops, the Chiang Rai Night Bazaar also boasts a bustling environment of entertainment. As twilight comes in, traditional dance performances and live music fill the air with melody and rhythm. The bazaar's entertainment sector is not merely an exhibition of artistic prowess, but also a location where cultural interaction occurs. Visitors have the ability to observe Thailand's rich performing arts heritage and even participate in interactive activities that promote an immersive understanding of local traditions.

It's not simply the commerce and entertainment that make the Chiang Rai Night Bazaar interesting; it's the interplay of these components against the backdrop of the city's historical and contemporary themes. The market is ideally positioned near the King Mengrai Monument, paying honor to the city's founder and affording visitors a historical context for their experiences. Furthermore, the bazaar's involvement in the local economy and the livelihoods of artists and sellers contributes to the ongoing story of Chiang Rai's growth and development.

For tourists wanting an authentic Thai experience, the Chiang Rai Night Bazaar provides an opportunity to mingle with the local population and acquire insights into their way of life. The bustling ambiance, the vast selection of items, the enticing flavors, and the engaging performances all combine together to create an immersive experience that lingers in the memory long after the visit.

Lopburi

Known as the "Monkey City" because of its playful residents, Lopburi boasts a rich history that extends back to the Dvaravati and Khmer civilizations, leaving behind a path of stunning architecture and old ruins. The most prominent site is the Phra Prang Sam Yot, an awe-inspiring Khmer-style temple filled with beautiful carvings and sculptures. The temple's magnificent mix of Hindu and Buddhist elements reflects the happy coexistence of diverse cultures in the region.

Another historical jewel is the Prang Khaek Temple, known for its well-preserved 13th-century sandstone shrine. This site provides a look into the Khmer architectural brilliance and their devotion to religious creativity. Additionally, the King Narai National Museum is a must-visit for history aficionados, showcasing an array of items that tell the account of Lopburi's illustrious past.

One of Lopburi's most odd and lovable traits is its colony of macaque monkeys that walk freely around the town. The monkeys have become a vital part of the local culture and are often identified with the spiritual heritage of the area. They are known to inhabit several temples and historical locations, like the Phra Prang Sam Yot, where tourists can see their amusing antics. Feeding the monkeys is a popular activity, giving a fascinating and participatory experience for tourists.

Lopburi's lively culture is also represented through its numerous festivals and events that honor the town's history and traditions. The Monkey Buffet Festival, conducted yearly, is a unique spectacle when local folks prepare a magnificent feast for the monkeys. This festival displays the town's harmonious relationship with its simian inhabitants and invites curious tourists from around the world.

Also, the Songkran event, the Thai New Year's celebration, is an enthusiastic water event that sees the town come alive with music, dancing, and water fights. This event provides a look into the lively and happy character of the local people.

No visit to Lopburi is complete without indulging in its wonderful cuisine. The town's cafes offer an array of traditional Thai meals, and one may appreciate authentic flavors that tickle the taste buds. From fragrant green curry to spicy papaya salad, the local food scene shows the varied influences that have influenced Thai culinary traditions.

While Lopburi is rich in history, it's also a lively modern town that offers a blend of old-world charm and contemporary amenities. Visitors can visit bustling marketplaces, indulge in shopping, and mingle with friendly people. This perfect blend of the past and present gives an engaging travel experience that displays the town's adaptation and tenacity over the years.

Phuket Old Town

Nestled on the southern coast of Thailand, the colorful and picturesque Phuket Old Town gives travelers a mesmerizing blend of history, culture, and architectural magnificence. The history of Phuket Old Town stretches back to the 19th century when it was a lively trading hub, welcoming merchants from many corners of the world. The architecture of the town bears tribute to this cosmopolitan heritage, showing a fascinating combination of Chinese, Portuguese, and Thai elements. Walking along the picturesque streets, travelers will be greeted by well-preserved Sino-Portuguese shophouses with their colorful façade, elaborate wooden shutters, and artistic woodwork. These architectural marvels provide a peek into the town's colonial past and make for an immersive historical experience.

Exploring Phuket Old Town isn't only about admiring buildings; it's also a journey into the cultural tapestry of the island. The district's rich blend of ethnicities is perhaps best visible in its cuisine. A tour through the bustling markets and eateries exposes a spectrum of flavors, from traditional Thai specialties to delightful Chinese and Peranakan cuisine. Travelers can tickle their taste buds with local favorites like "mee hoon gaeng" (rice noodle curry) and "oh tao" (fried oyster omelet), delivering a true gourmet excursion.

As twilight descends over Phuket Old Town, the area transforms into an ethereal fantasy. The weekly Lard Yai pedestrian street market comes alive, presenting a diversity of handicrafts, apparel, and art, with street performances and cultural exhibitions. It's a perfect time to connect with residents, observe traditional Thai dancing, and even participate in hands-on workshops that provide insights into the town's cultural legacy.

Museums and cultural centers dot the landscape of the Old Town, offering in-depth glimpses into the island's history and traditions. The Thai Hua Museum, built in a former Chinese-language school, showcases the journey of Phuket's different populations. Displays of tin mining, traditional attire, and rituals provide a full insight into the island's past.

For those with a taste for spirituality, the Old Town has a variety of magnificently embellished temples. The Jui Tui Shrine, dedicated to the Taoist deity of medicine, exudes an impression of tranquillity amidst the bustling streets. The Shrine's magnificent architecture, bright sculptures, and exuberant ceremonies provide an insight into the local spiritual practices.

Phuket Old Town's appeal isn't restricted to its daytime activities. The town's nightlife offers a unique blend of old and new, as ancient buildings create a picturesque backdrop for modern clubs, cafes, and boutique shops. Rooftop bars offer panoramic views of the town, allowing visitors to soak in the ambiance while sipping on a delicious cocktail.

Conclusion

Thailand is a country that beckons vacationers with its varied range of attractions. From bustling metropolises to quiet beaches, from ancient ruins to colorful marketplaces, the country offers an immersive experience that mixes rich history, cultural legacy, and natural beauty. Thailand's ability to perfectly integrate heritage with contemporary provides a tapestry of experiences that leave an everlasting impact on every visitor. Whether you're drawn to its beautiful temples, bustling markets, calm beaches, or adrenaline-pumping activities, Thailand certainly has something for everyone, making it a must-visit destination for any ardent traveler eager to see the beauty and wonder of Southeast Asia.

Top Cuisine to Try Out

Thailand is also recognized for its diverse and wonderful cuisine. With a complex blend of flavors, textures, and aromatic spices, Thai food has garnered a global reputation. For any traveler visiting this interesting country, exploring the native cuisine is a must. From street cuisine to gourmet dining, Thailand provides a diversity of foods that tickle the taste senses and deliver a real gastronomic experience. Here are popular foods that travelers can sample in Thailand:

Pad Thai

Pad Thai is an iconic street food stir-fried noodle meal that normally consists of thin rice noodles, shrimp, chicken, tofu, eggs, and a variety of veggies, all sautéed together in a wok. The meal is noted for its sweet, sour, salty, and umami characteristics, obtained through the combination of important ingredients such as tamarind paste, fish sauce, palm sugar, and lime. These components form a harmonious balance that thrills the taste buds and gives a pleasing experience.

The origins of Pad Thai stretch back to the 1930s when the Thai government tried to establish a sense of national identity and solidarity. At that time, Thailand was undergoing a phase of modernization, and the government attempted to boost the consumption of rice noodles, an indigenous staple, to decrease rice consumption owing to a rice crisis. Pad Thai arose as a solution, merging local ingredients with Chinese-inspired cooking techniques. Over time, it evolved to accommodate diverse proteins and cater to different tastes.

While Pad Thai may be found in restaurants around the country, some of the tastiest versions are generally offered by street sellers. These sellers take pride in mastering their recipes and often add their own distinctive tweaks to the original meal, making the street food experience a vital element of Thailand's gastronomic scene. Tourists are urged to tour local markets and food booths to sample authentic Pad Thai produced by professional vendors who have polished their technique over decades.

The process of producing Pad Thai is an art in itself. The wok heats up to high temperatures, ensuring that the items are cooked rapidly and keep their individual flavors and textures. The meal is commonly served with crushed peanuts, bean sprouts, and fresh herbs, giving a delicious crunch and aromatic aroma.

Partaking in Pad Thai isn't only about gratifying your taste senses; it's also an immersing cultural experience. Watching the expert sellers deftly toss ingredients in a sizzling wok, breathing the aromatic fragrances of the meal as its being produced, and tasting the sophisticated blend of flavors all combine for a genuinely unforgettable encounter with Thai cuisine.

Tom Yum Goong (Spicy Shrimp Soup)

Tom Yum Goong, generally referred to simply as Tom Yum, is a traditional Thai meal recognized for its fascinating blend of flavors and aromatic profile. This popular soup encompasses the essence of Thai cuisine, mixing spicy, sour, and savory flavors to produce a harmonious and thrilling taste experience.

At its foundation, Tom Yum Goong is a hot and sour soup that prominently utilizes shrimp as its main protein source. The name itself represents the prominent characteristics: "Tom" translates to boiling, "Yum" alludes to the spicy and sour flavors, and "Goong" symbolizes shrimp. The soup is recognized by its brilliant reddish-orange hue, a result of infusing the broth with chili peppers.

Lemongrass, galangal (a relative of ginger), and kaffir lime leaves form the trio of fragrant herbs that establish the foundation for the soup's characteristic aroma. These components are often gently bruised before being added to the broth, releasing their essential oils and imbuing the soup with their identifiable essence.

To create the broth, the herbs and spices are cooked in a base of chicken or shrimp stock, enabling the flavors to blend. A considerable amount of fresh chiles gives fire to the soup, while lime juice imparts the crucial sourness. The combination of these two different flavors provides a delicious taste that dances on the palette.

Plump shrimp are a feature of Tom Yum Goong, signifying Thailand's rich seaside cuisine. The shrimp are simmered in the fragrant broth until they turn pink and soft, absorbing the subtle aromas of the soup.

Vegetables including mushrooms, tomatoes, and onions are added to enhance the soup's texture and flavor profile. The final touch of fish sauce and a dab of sugar balances the dish, combining the powerful flavors into a well-rounded feeling.

Tom Yum Goong is not simply a gustatory treat but it carries cultural significance. It embodies the Thai principle of harmonizing the five primary flavors: spicy, sour, sweet, salty, and bitter. This harmony is supposed to generate a sense of stability in both the body and mind.

This renowned Thai cuisine is consumed in many settings, from lowly street food booths to upmarket establishments. Its popularity has transcended borders, making it a standard in Thai restaurants worldwide. Tom Yum Goong reflects the heart of Thai cuisine, a symphony of flavors that encapsulates the country's culinary tradition, innovation, and enthusiasm for robust tastes. For any tourist to Thailand, a hot bowl of Tom Yum Goong is a required study of the country's varied gastronomic environment.

Green Curry

Green Curry, or "Gaeng Keow Wan" in Thai, is a typical meal that embodies the robust flavors and aromatic spices of Thai cuisine.

The brilliant green hue of the curry is generated from the copious use of fresh green chilies, which are mashed together with a variety of fragrant herbs and spices such as lemongrass, galangal, garlic, and kaffir lime leaves. This aromatic paste acts as the core of the meal, infusing it with a deep layer of taste. The paste is sautéed in a skillet until its aroma envelops the senses, offering an intriguing start to the meal.

One can tailor their green curry experience by selecting a protein of their choice, which is commonly chicken, beef, pork, shrimp, or tofu. The protein is added to the simmering curry paste, enabling the flavors to merge together. The creaminess of the curry owes itself to the use of rich coconut milk, which tempers the spiciness of the dish while producing a sumptuous texture.

The curry is traditionally served with jasmine rice, allowing guests to experience the strong flavors of the dish while enjoying the soft, fragrant rice. Garnishes such as Thai basil leaves, sliced red chilies, and sometimes a drizzle of coconut cream are added to improve the dish's visual appeal and culinary diversity.

Green Curry is more than simply a gourmet joy; it symbolizes the balance of flavors that Thai cuisine is known for — the harmonious interplay of spicy, sweet, salty, and herbal undertones. It also symbolizes the nation's emphasis on using fresh ingredients and carefully picked spices to produce a really immersive dining experience.

Partaking in Green Curry in Thailand offers travelers a unique glimpse into the country's culinary legacy and cultural richness. It's a dish that epitomizes the essence of Thailand – vivid, bold, and complex. Enjoying it in local eateries or street food vendors delivers an authentic experience that goes beyond taste, connecting visitors to the heart of Thai culture.

Som Tum (Papaya Salad)

Som Tum, generally known as Papaya Salad, illustrates the wonderful balance of sweet, sour, spicy, and salty flavors that Thai cuisine is famed for. This dish, originating from the northeastern part of Thailand, has become a popular staple in Thai street cuisine as well as restaurant menus worldwide.

At its foundation, Som Tum is a salad composed mostly of unripe green papaya. The papaya is shredded or julienned, providing a delicate yet crunchy basis. The salad's unique flavors are obtained from a vivid dressing prepared from a blend of ingredients such as lime juice, fish sauce, palm sugar, and chiles. The balance of these elements provides the foundation of the dish, ensuring that no single flavor overpowers the others.

One of the most remarkable elements of Som Tum is its adaptability. There are different regional and ingredient variations, each lending a unique edge to the dish. For instance, Som Tum Thai contains peanuts, tomatoes, and dried shrimp, improving the texture and taste. On the other hand, Som Tum Lao, which derives from the northeastern Isaan region, may incorporate fermented fish sauce and fermented crab, boosting the umami and depth of taste.

The preparation of Som Tum is a show in itself. Traditionally, the components are blended in a huge mortar and pestle, where they are mashed together. This approach not only blends the flavors but also releases the essential oils from the components, resulting in an aromatic and visually beautiful dish. The act of hammering also plays a part in breaking down the papaya's fibers, helping it to absorb the dressing more effectively.

Som Tum has garnered international recognition due to its mix of flavors, healthiness, and colorful presentation. It embodies the essence of Thai cuisine by integrating the four main flavors, providing a harmonious and enjoyable meal. Tourists are typically lured to the sensory experience of watching the food being produced directly in front of them, as well as the anticipation of tasting the burst of sensations on their tongue.

In Thailand, Som Tum is a dish that encompasses the spirit of Thai street food culture, enabling travelers to engage in the sensory experience and savor an authentic flavor of Thailand. Whether consumed as a refreshing appetizer, a zesty side dish, or a fiery main meal, Som Tum continues to win the hearts and taste buds of people throughout the world.

Massaman Curry

Massaman Curry is a wonderful Thai meal, noted for its harmonious balance of tastes, has its origins in Southern Thailand but exhibits influences from Persian, Malay, and Indian cuisines.

The core of Massaman Curry resides in its unique blend of ingredients. Tender chunks of meat, frequently beef or chicken, are cooked in a luxuriously creamy and aromatic sauce. This sauce owes its flavor diversity to a multitude of spices, with main actors including cinnamon, cloves, cardamom, and star anise. These spices not only infuse the curry with warmth but also produce a depth of taste that is both soothing and intriguing.

One of the most unique characteristics of Massaman Curry is its combination of peanuts and potatoes. These components give a great tactile contrast to the soft meat, and they absorb the rich flavors of the curry, becoming sumptuous and gratifying. Additionally, the meal is typically topped with crispy shallots and fresh cilantro, improving its visual appeal and adding a burst of freshness to each bite.

Beyond its culinary charm, Massaman Curry bears cultural significance in Thailand. The curry's origin is said to be related to the Muslim community in Southern Thailand, which explains the Persian and Malay influences present in its ingredients and spices. Over time, Massaman Curry has evolved into a beloved Thai dish, demonstrating the country's ability to absorb and adopt foreign influences while infusing them with a unique Thai twist.

For travelers, relishing a plate of Massaman Curry offers a tantalizing insight into Thailand's unique cultural tapestry. It's a meal that seamlessly crosses the gap between tradition and innovation, symbolizing the nation's openness to new culinary experiences while keeping entrenched in its legacy. Whether savored at a street-side stall, a neighborhood cafe, or a fine dining restaurant, Massaman Curry guarantees a wonderful voyage of flavor and aroma.

Pad See Ew (Stir-Fried Noodles)

Originating from Chinese culinary traditions that have merged effortlessly with Thai ingredients and techniques, Pad See Ew translates to "stir-fried soy sauce" in English. This recipe is characterized by its simplicity, however, it features an explosion of tastes that accentuates the balance of sweet, salty, and umami ingredients. The meal is often cooked with large rice noodles, which offer a delightful chewiness to each bite.

The core of Pad See Ew is its stir-frying technique. Traditionally made in a wok over high heat, the procedure results in a wonderful smokey scent and slightly scorched edges on the noodles. This cooking method offers a characteristic wok hei, or "breath of the wok," which enriches the whole experience of the dish.

One of the main components of Pad See Ew is the choice of protein. While chicken and pig are popular alternatives, versions using beef, shrimp, or tofu are also generally loved. The protein is often marinated in soy sauce and other seasonings before being stir-fried, adding depth to the overall flavor.

The marriage of tastes in Pad See Ew is further enhanced by the inclusion of fresh veggies. Chinese broccoli, known as "gai lan," is a typical choice, adding a somewhat bitter and earthy taste that complements the savory sauce. The vegetables are cooked to retain their crispness, creating a lovely contrast to the silky noodles.

The sauce itself is a critical aspect that connects all the components together. A combination of soy sauce, oyster sauce, and sometimes black soy sauce creates the basis, giving the dish a rich and delicious umami flavor. The sauce is sweetened with a bit of sugar, balancing the saltiness and imparting a note of sweetness to the tongue. The meal may also contain a dash of vinegar or lime juice to cut through the richness, offering a refreshing acidity.

Chilies are often incorporated to offer a kick of heat, allowing customers to modify the spice level to their desire. Crushed peanuts or a sprinkle of white pepper can be used as garnishes, giving texture and an extra layer of flavor depth.

Khao Pad (Fried Rice)

Khao Pad, commonly known as Fried Rice, is a renowned and ubiquitous dish in Thailand, cherished for its tasty blend of ingredients and adaptability. At its foundation, Khao Pad is a basic yet lively recipe that comprises cooked rice stir-fried with a multitude of toppings. The recipe often begins with jasmine rice, a fragrant long-grain variety that provides the appropriate base. The rice is often pre-cooked and cooled to ensure individual grains won't clump together during frying.

What actually elevates Khao Pad is the mix of ingredients that infuse it with a blast of flavors. Common components include chopped veggies like onions, bell peppers, and carrots, which offer both crunch and color. A choice of protein, such as chicken, shrimp, pork, or tofu, gives weight and depth to the dish. It's not uncommon to use leftover meat, making Khao Pad a practical way to repurpose materials.

Thai cuisine's unique flavors play a key part in enhancing the taste. Garlic, chile, and sometimes basil are sautéed to infuse the dish with aromatic spice. A flavorful blend of fish sauce, soy sauce, and oyster sauce is drizzled in, creating that signature umami punch.

What actually differentiates Khao Pad is the interplay of textures and the chef's ingenuity. From the soft, fluffy grains of rice to the tender bits of protein and the sharpness of veggies, each taste delivers a pleasant contrast. The dish is generally served with a wedge of lime and a few slices of cucumber, which offer refreshing tanginess to cut through the richness.

Khao Pad is also a canvas for culinary innovation. Variations vary, adapting to dietary choices and regional factors. Pineapple Fried Rice, for instance, contains pineapple pieces for sweetness, while the spicy Basil Fried Rice showcases the aromatic herb's distinct flavor. Regardless of the rendition, Khao Pad is often crowned with a fried egg, its sunny yolk adding a creamy aspect to the dish.

A truly Thai gastronomic experience, Khao Pad epitomizes the country's ideal of blending varied flavors and ingredients. Beyond its deliciousness, the dish reflects Thai culture's community ethos, as it's regularly shared among friends and family. Whether consumed at a street-side stall, a simple cafe, or a fine-dining establishment, Khao Pad encompasses the essence of Thai cuisine, making it a must-try for every traveler seeking a comprehensive immersion in Thailand's culinary traditions.

Tom Kha Gai (Chicken Coconut Soup)

Tom Kha Gai, which translates to "chicken galangal soup," is noted for its perfect combination of sweet, sour, savory, and spicy elements. The soup is usually created by cooking soft chicken chunks, aromatic galangal (a ginger-like root), lemongrass, and kaffir lime leaves in a fragrant coconut milk broth. This mixture results in a silky texture that covers the palette while offering a rush of vivid tastes.

The soup's flavor profile is determined by the harmonic interplay of its major ingredients. The galangal offers a subtle lemony and earthy taste, while lemongrass imparts a zesty and invigorating scent. Kaffir lime leaves infuse a lemony aroma, while Thai chili peppers give a moderate rush of heat. The coconut milk, a characteristic Thai ingredient, balances the soup with its creamy sweetness, functioning as a backdrop to the more strong flavors.

Tom Kha Gai is a comfort meal that transcends seasons. The warm and calming broth makes it a great choice on cooler days, while its lively flavors and fresh ingredients appeal to the senses during warmer months. Its variety extends to nutritional choices as well, with varieties that cater to vegans and seafood fans.

One can commonly find Tom Kha Gai served with a side of steaming jasmine rice, which serves to reduce the soup's spiciness and complements its creamy texture. The presentation is sometimes embellished with a sprinkle of fresh cilantro, which gives a bit of herbal aroma and a flash of color.

While Tom Kha Gai is enjoyed across Thailand, its origin is considered to be based in central Thailand, with its variants and popularity spreading throughout the country and beyond. In addition to its wonderful taste, the soup carries cultural value as a depiction of Thai culinary talent, integrating traditional ingredients and cooking techniques in a harmonious manner.

For tourists wanting an authentic taste of Thailand, Tom Kha Gai is a must-try dish that encompasses the essence of the country's flavors and customs. Its delicate combination of ingredients and flavors, coupled with its enticing scent, gives it a remarkable culinary experience that encapsulates the heart and spirit of Thai cuisine.

Pla Rad Prik (Fried Fish and Chili-Sauce)

At the center of Pla Rad Prik is the fish itself, sometimes a whole fish like snapper or sea bass. The fish is painstakingly scored and deep-fried until the skin is crispy and the flesh soft. This initial phase not only creates textural contrast but also allows the chili sauce to permeate into the fish, creating a perfect marriage of flavors.

The star of the show is clearly the chili sauce. Bursting with heat and flavor, it's a mixture of red and green chilies, garlic, shallots, and typically fermented shrimp paste. These ingredients are mashed into a fragrant paste and then stir-fried to release their scents. The sauce's spiciness is reduced by the addition of palm sugar, providing a delicate balance between blazing heat and gentle sweetness. A dab of fish sauce and lime juice adds depth and zing, embodying the signature Thai sweet-sour-salty taste.

Pla Rad Prik's presentation is a feast for the eyes as well. The deep-fried fish is elegantly presented on a dish, topped generously with the glossy chili sauce. Sprinkles of fresh cilantro and thin strips of kaffir lime leaves not only enhance the dish's visual attractiveness but also infuse it with aromatic herbal overtones.

This dish carries cultural value also, as it shows the Thai emphasis on community dining. Pla Rad Prik is generally consumed in groups, where sharing becomes a vital part of the experience. The delicious aroma of the chili sauce, the sizzling sound of the fish as it arrives at the table, and the collective pleasure of its rich flavors create a sense of camaraderie and celebration.

In Thailand, Pla Rad Prik can be found in street stalls, neighborhood eateries, and posh restaurants. Its appeal has transcended borders, making it a favorite among both residents and tourists seeking a genuine Thai gastronomic journey.

Larb (Spicy Minced Meat Salad)

Larb is a cuisine that revolves around the harmonious marriage of minced beef, fragrant herbs, toasted rice powder, and a blend of invigorating flavors. The choice of meat can vary, ranging from chicken, pork, or even fish, with each protein giving its particular taste to the dish. The beef is normally cooked, minced, and then mixed with an aromatic blend of shallots, mint leaves, cilantro, and green onions. This combination of herbs gives a fresh and energetic flavor, while also presenting a dramatic contrast to the dish's spiciness.

The fiery characteristic of larb originates from the copious use of chilies and the incendiary kick of prik khua, a roasted chili paste. The chilies not only give a punch of heat but also fill the meal with a richness of flavors that dance on the taste buds. The balance of heat is further adjusted with the addition of fish sauce, lime juice, and sometimes a touch of palm sugar.

These ingredients collide to create a symphony of flavors that is at once savory, spicy, sour, and somewhat sweet.

A characteristic component of larb is khao khua, roasted rice powder. This key addition provides texture, depth, and a slight nuttiness to the meal. Rice is toasted till golden brown, then pounded to a coarse powder. This powder not only enriches the overall eating experience but also helps absorb some of the flavorful fluids from the meat and herbs, providing a gratifying blend of tastes and sensations.

Larb is commonly served with a variety of complementing vegetables, including as cabbage leaves, cucumber slices, and Thai basil, which give a cooling and crisp contrast to the heaviness of the minced meat mixture. These accompaniments not only enhance the aesthetic attractiveness of the dish but also serve a refreshing palate cleanser between mouthfuls of the highly flavorful salad.

Part of larb's charm resides in its adaptability. While the essential components remain stable, variations can be found across Thailand's unique culinary terrain. In some locations, larb may feature raw or blanched vegetables, adding an added layer of crunch and freshness. Additionally, the level of spiciness can be modified to individual preferences, ensuring that each plate of larb caters to a wide spectrum of heat tolerance.

For the adventurous traveler looking to go on a culinary voyage through Thailand, sampling larb is a rite of passage. Its rich flavors and numerous layers offer a real peek into the heart of Thai cuisine, showing the nation's passion for crafting dishes that are equally stimulating and harmonious. From the bustling streets of Bangkok to the humble food stalls in remote regions, Larb's ubiquity emphasizes its reputation as a cherished and quintessential Thai cuisine.

Khao Niew Mamuang (Mango Sticky Rice)

Khao Niew Mamuang, commonly known as Mango Sticky Rice, is a scrumptious and classic Thai dish that tantalizes the taste buds of locals and tourists alike. Khao Niew Mamuang consists of three primary components: sticky rice, ripe mango slices, and a sweet coconut milk sauce. The recipe starts with glutinous rice, which is soaked, steamed, and then gently blended with coconut milk, sugar, and a touch of salt. This method lends a slight sweetness and a peculiar sticky feel to the rice, making it a great substrate for the other ingredients.

The star of the show, ripe mango, is delicately cut and artfully laid above the bed of sticky rice. The mango's rich, succulent flesh contrasts nicely with the chewy rice, providing a lovely interplay of textures. The sweetness of the mango enriches the flavors of the dish, while its vivid color adds an appealing visual component.

To complete the outfit, a fragrant and creamy coconut milk sauce is drizzled over the mango and rice. This sauce is produced by gradually boiling coconut milk, sugar, and a bit of salt. Its silky richness not only enriches the overall taste but also provides a harmonious balance to the sweetness of the mango and rice.

Khao Niew Mamuang is not simply a dessert; it's a sensory experience that encapsulates the essence of Thai food. Its blend of flavors symbolizes the country's culinary concept of harmonizing sweet, salty, and creamy ingredients in each bite. The meal is not limited to high-end restaurants; street vendors across Thailand skilfully create and serve it, assuring its accessibility to all.

Beyond its culinary allure, Khao Niew Mamuang is rich in cultural significance. Mangoes are adored in Thai culture as a symbol of abundance and fortune, making this dish a popular sight during festivals and celebrations. It's also a testament to the country's concentration on using local, seasonal products to produce recipes that capture the character of the region.

For tourists, engaging in Khao Niew Mamuang delivers an authentic sense of Thailand. It's a cuisine that crosses language borders, allowing travelers to engage with the local culture through their taste sensations. Whether consumed at a street-side stall or a high-end restaurant, this dessert is a must-try for anybody wishing to appreciate Thailand's culinary wonders. So, whether you're a cuisine connoisseur or an adventurous tourist, make sure to experience the delicious symphony of flavors that is Khao Niew Mamuang.

Conclusion

Exploring Thai cuisine is not just about enjoying the food but also witnessing the cultural tapestry that defines the country. From the lively street markets to the posh restaurants, Thailand provides a broad choice of dishes that cater to every appetite. With its harmonious balance of flavors and textures, Thai food invites travelers to embark on a gastronomic trip that represents the country's rich history, geography, and cultural influences. So, whether you're tasting the classic Pad Thai or relishing the rich flavors of Tom Yum Goong, each bite is a step closer to comprehending the heart and soul of Thailand.

Best Time To Visit

When planning a visit to this Southeast Asian treasure, choosing the ideal time to go is vital to make the most of your trip. The climate and Thailand events play a vital impact in deciding the optimal time for your trip.

Seasons and Climate

Thailand experiences three primary seasons: the hot season, the rainy season, and the cold season. The optimal time to visit mostly depends on your taste for the weather and the activities you wish to engage in.

Cool Season (November to February): This is often regarded as the ideal season to visit Thailand. The weather is fairly mild, with daytime temperatures ranging from 20°C to 30°C (68°F to 86°F). This season is particularly popular among travelers because of the favorable weather, making it excellent for outdoor activities and exploring the country's sites. The chilly season also corresponds with the peak tourist season, so be prepared for increased crowds and higher rates.

Hot Season (March to May): The hot season in Thailand is characterized by high temperatures that can reach up to 40°C (104°F). While it might be fairly warm, it's also the best season for beach fans and sun-seekers. Islands like Phuket, Koh Samui, and Krabi were popular destinations during this period. Keep in mind that some inland places can become unbearably hot, so plan your schedule accordingly.

Rainy Season (June to October): The rainy season, also known as the monsoon season, is when Thailand receives

150

most of its annual rainfall. While the weather can be unpredictable with occasional torrential downpours, it's also the period when the country's lush surroundings are at their most brilliant. This season is perfect for budget tourists, as hotels and activities are more reasonable due to lesser demand.

Festivals and Events

Thailand's cultural festivals and events are a big magnet for tourists. The time of your visit can coincide with these festivals, allowing you a unique peek into the local traditions and way of life.

Regional Considerations

Thailand's diverse topography means that the best time to travel can vary depending on the place you wish to see.

Northern Thailand: The chilly season (November to February) is great for visiting northern cities like Chiang Mai and Chiang Rai. The weather is comfortable for exploring temples, trekking, and experiencing local hill cultures.

Central Thailand: Bangkok and the central region are best visited during the cold and dry season (November to February) when the weather is most pleasant. Avoid the wet season if you wish to see the city comfortably.

Southern Thailand: For beach lovers, the dry season (November to April) is great for visiting islands like Phuket, Koh Phi Phi, and Koh Lanta. The rainy season (May to October) can bring severe rainfall, but costs are lower and the scenery is lush.

Conclusion

The best time to visit Thailand depends on your preferences for weather, festivals, and the locations you wish to explore. Each season offers a unique experience, whether you're seeking a vibrant cultural festival, beach relaxation, or outdoor excursions. By considering these elements, you may design your vacation to ensure a memorable and delightful visit to the Land of Smiles.

Traveling Itinerary

With Thailand's numerous attractions, hospitable locals, and wonderful cuisine, it has become a top choice for travelers seeking an outstanding vacation experience. Whether you have one week or two to spare, this itinerary will guide you through the must-see locations and activities in Thailand. Here's a thorough 1 and 2-week vacation plan for Thailand.

1-Week Itinerary: Exploring Bangkok and Chiang Mai

Day 1: Arrive in Bangkok, check into your hotel, and get acquainted with the city. Spend the afternoon exploring the Grand Palace, Wat Phra Kaew (Temple of the Emerald Buddha), and Wat Pho (Temple of the Reclining Buddha).

Day 2: Visit the lively Chatuchak Weekend Market, then enjoy a boat trip along the Chao Phraya River. In the evening, discover the bustling street food scene in Chinatown.

Day 3: Take a day journey to Ayutthaya, a historic city with spectacular ruins. Return to Bangkok and visit Jim Thompson House and explore Sukhumvit Road for shopping.

Day 4: Immerse yourself in Thai culture by taking a traditional Thai cooking lesson. In the afternoon, visit the Erawan Shrine and shop in the MBK Center.

Day 5: Depart for Chiang Mai. Explore the lively Night Bazaar and try local delicacies.

Day 6: Visit Doi Suthep Temple and enjoy panoramic views of the city. In the afternoon, explore the Old City and its temples.

Day 7: Embark on an elephant sanctuary tour and mingle with these gentle giants. Wrap up your Chiang Mai tour with a pleasant Thai massage.

2-Week Itinerary: Beaches, Culture, and Islands

Days 1-7: Bangkok and Chiang Mai (Same as 1-week itinerary)

Day 8: Arrive in Phuket and check into your coastal resort. Relax on Patong Beach and discover Patong's bustling nightlife.

Day 9: Take a day trip to Phi Phi Islands for snorkeling, swimming, and beach relaxing.

Day 10: Explore Old Phuket Town for its attractive Sino-Portuguese architecture and interesting street art.

Day 11: Travel to Krabi and settle into your resort. Visit Railay Beach and discover its limestone cliffs and lovely waves.

Day 12: Venture to the magnificent Phang Nga Bay, noted for its limestone karsts. You can explore sea caves and enjoy kayaking.

Day 13: Arrive in Koh Samui and unwind on the gorgeous Chaweng Beach. In the evening, experience the bustling Fisherman's Village.

Day 14: Enjoy a day trip to Ang Thong Marine Park for snorkeling, kayaking, and trekking. Alternatively, you can choose to unwind on the beach.

Conclusion

Whether you have one or two weeks, Thailand provides a varied choice of experiences. From seeing the rich history and culture of Bangkok and Chiang Mai to relaxing on the magnificent beaches of Phuket, Krabi, and Koh Samui, you'll get to immerse yourself in the beauty, adventure, and peace that this incredible country has to offer. Remember to adjust the plan to your interests and pace, and always take some time to simply absorb the local ambiance and flavors.

Visiting On a Budget

With some intelligent planning and a little flexibility, you may experience the pleasures of this Southeast Asian jewel without draining your wallet. Here's how to visit Thailand on a budget:

Affordable Accommodation

Thailand offers a wide selection of hotel options that fit varied budgets. From budget hostels to guesthouses and even modest boutique hotels, you can discover comfortable places to stay without overspending. Booking in advance and selecting slightly off-the-beaten-path locales will help you score better bargains.

Local Transport

Getting around Thailand doesn't have to be expensive. Opt for local transportation like tuk-tuks, songthaews (shared taxis), and local buses instead of private cabs. Trains and sleeper buses are other affordable solutions for traveling between cities. Consider installing local ride-hailing apps to guarantee you're getting fair charges.

Street Food Delights

One of the attractions of visiting Thailand is its excellent street food scene. Indulge in traditional Thai foods at local street booths and marketplaces. Not only is this an economical way to eat delicious cuisine, but it's also an engaging cultural experience.

Bargain Shopping

Whether you're seeking souvenirs, clothing, or handicrafts, Thailand's markets are a treasure mine for budget shoppers.

Hone your haggling abilities to get the finest discounts at marketplaces like Chatuchak in Bangkok or the Night Bazaar in Chiang Mai.

Free and Low-Cost Activities
Thailand offers a plethora of free or low-cost activities. Explore historic temples, relax on magnificent beaches, or soak in the natural beauty of areas like Erawan National Park or the limestone cliffs of Railay Beach. Many cities also organize affordable or free cultural events and festivals.

Cultural Etiquette
Respecting local customs and traditions can save you from unneeded charges. For instance, dressing modestly when visiting temples can help you avoid renting or buying cover-up apparel. Learning a few basic Thai phrases can also increase your interactions with locals.

Island Hopping on a Budget
While Thailand's islands are popular tourist destinations, you can still enjoy them without overspending. Choose less popular islands like Koh Lanta or Koh Tao, where accommodation and activities tend to be more budget-friendly.

Budget-Friendly Excursions
Participating in group trips or excursions can frequently be cheaper than organizing everything alone. These trips might take you to popular destinations and activities like snorkeling, hiking, or touring local towns.

Off-Peak Travel
Timing your travel to Thailand during the shoulder seasons (spring and fall) will help you escape the peak tourist crowds

and expensive rates. Flight and accommodation offers are more probable during these times.

Limit Alcohol and Entertainment Expenses
Alcohol and partying can drastically inflate your bills. Enjoying local beverages and limiting your nights out will help you preserve your budget. Instead, engage in more daytime activities and enjoy the cultural diversity of the country.

Cash vs. Cards
While credit and debit cards are generally accepted, certain smaller companies may prefer cash. Carrying a mix of both can assist you in negotiating diverse scenarios without incurring excessive transaction fees.

Travel Insurance
Though it can seem contradictory to spending less, investing in comprehensive travel insurance is a sensible choice. It can safeguard you from unforeseen medical expenditures, travel cancellations, or theft, ensuring your budget remains intact.

Conclusion
A budget-conscious trip to Thailand is perfectly achievable with careful planning and informed judgments. Embrace the local culture, savor economical street food, and choose cost-effective accommodations and transit options. By establishing a balance between exploration and budgeting, you may build lasting memories of Thailand's stunning scenery, dynamic cities, and kind hospitality without emptying your wallet.

Getting Around

Thailand offers a diversity of transportation alternatives to help travelers navigate its different regions. Whether you're touring the bustling streets of Bangkok, the peaceful coasts of Phuket, or the ancient ruins of Ayutthaya, here's a full guide to traveling around Thailand.

Tuk-tuks and Songthaews
In urban regions like Bangkok and Chiang Mai, tuk-tuks (three-wheeled motorized taxis) and songthaews (shared pickup trucks with bench seats) are iconic and provide a quintessential Thai experience. While tuk-tuks are great for short distances, songthaews are more practical for group transport and slightly longer trips within city borders.

Public Buses
Major cities have significant public bus networks, offering budget-friendly options for passengers. Bangkok's air-conditioned buses give comfortable trips around the city. Long-distance buses are also accessible for intercity travel, making it a cheap method to explore other locations.

Skytrains and Subways
Bangkok boasts an effective public transit infrastructure, including the BTS Skytrain and MRT metro. These solutions are great for avoiding the city's renowned traffic bottlenecks while conveniently linking essential regions. They are especially beneficial for reaching renowned tourist attractions and retail centers.

Ferries and Longtail Boats

For island hopping and coastal exploring, Thailand's network of ferries and longtail boats is important. Whether you're island hopping in the Gulf of Thailand or exploring the Andaman Sea, these boats provide a gorgeous and often exhilarating form of transit.

Domestic Flights

For crossing vast distances fast, domestic flights are a convenient option. With multiple airports serving diverse destinations, you may easily explore isolated areas or links between big cities.

Motorbike Rentals

For those wanting independence and flexibility, motorbike rentals are a popular alternative, especially in destinations like Phuket, Koh Samui, and Chiang Mai. However, be cautious and verify you have the right license and proper safety gear.

Trains

Thailand's train network is a wonderful method to tour the nation at a leisurely pace. The train journey from Bangkok to Chiang Mai, known as the "Northern Line," is particularly famous for presenting spectacular vistas of the landscape. Trains offer numerous classes, from basic seats to sleeper cabins.

Rental Cars

While navigating Thailand's major cities can be tough, hiring a car can be a useful alternative for exploring less populated locations. It's an excellent choice for road trips through the countryside, especially in northern regions.

Ride-Sharing Apps

Uber used to operate in Thailand, however, it has been supplanted by local ride-sharing services like Grab. These apps are convenient for brief journeys, especially when language problems can be a worry.

Walking and Cycling

Exploring on foot or by bicycle is a wonderful way to immerse yourself in the local culture. Many cities have pedestrian-friendly sections, and bike trips are popular in locations like Sukhothai, famed for its ancient park.

Conclusion

Thailand offers a varied assortment of transportation options, catering to various preferences and budgets. From the turmoil of tuk-tuks in bustling marketplaces to the tranquillity of longtail boat trips through calm islands, every means of transportation contributes its own particular flavor to the Thai experience. As you plan your tour, consider a mix of these options to truly experience the beauty and diversity that Thailand has to offer. Just remember to prioritize safety, plan your trips, and be open to the adventures that await in every corner of this lovely country.

Shopping for Souvenirs

When it comes to shopping for souvenirs, few countries can rival the wide and lively options of Thailand. This Southeast Asian treasure has also established a niche for itself as a paradise for souvenir enthusiasts. From lively markets to high-end boutiques, Thailand provides a kaleidoscope of alternatives for travelers eager to take a piece of its magic home with them.

Shopping for souvenirs in Thailand is more than just obtaining material goods; it's an opportunity to immerse oneself in the country's cultural tapestry. Traditional crafts, rich artwork, and distinctive designs are widespread in Thai souvenirs, making them more than just baubles, but tangible recollections of a wonderful experience.

Markets

For a real shopping experience, travelers should head to the lively markets that are dotted across Thailand. The Chatuchak Weekend Market in Bangkok is a must-visit, having over 8,000 stalls where visitors can purchase everything from handcrafted crafts to clothing and local foods. Another gem is the Chiang Mai Night Bazaar which we have highlighted in the tourist attraction section, a refuge for arts and crafts, jewelry, and textiles. These markets are not just a shopper's delight but also a cultural experience, with brilliant colors, energetic bargaining, and a combination of scents and noises.

Artisanal Crafts

Thailand's rich cultural legacy is reflected in its handmade crafts, which have been passed down through centuries. One of the most sought-after souvenirs is traditional Thai silk, woven in elaborate designs and brilliant colors. Visitors will also find beautiful pottery covered with elaborate designs, reflecting the country's artistic talent. The art of wood carving, shown in products like complex figurines and elegant furniture, is another tribute to Thailand's artistry.

Local Delicacies
Souvenirs should not be confined to material goods; Thailand's exquisite food industry offers a choice of tasty souvenirs. Packets of aromatic Thai spices, exotic herbs, and savory sauces are a terrific way to bring a taste of Thailand back home. Additionally, the famed Thai rice wines, including Sangsom and Mekhong, encapsulate the essence of the country's flavors and spirits.

Gemstones and Jewelry
Thailand is renowned for its gemstone trade, particularly its high-quality rubies and sapphires. Jewelry fans can explore specialist boutiques to acquire magnificent pieces set in various patterns. The city of Chanthaburi is famed for its gem markets, where both raw gemstones and skillfully created jewelry are available, typically at competitive costs.

Floating Markets
Floating markets are a prominent aspect of Thailand's shopping scene. These markets are not just about buying but also about witnessing the traditional way of life along the country's intricate network of canals. Damnoen Saduak Floating Market near Bangkok is a popular alternative, offering a diversity of fruits, vegetables, handicrafts, and even prepared dishes, all offered from boats floating on the lake.

Modern Boutiques

While traditional markets offer a look into the Thai past, the country's major cities also appeal to tourists seeking contemporary and luxury souvenirs. Cities like Bangkok feature high-end stores and shopping centers selling luxury labels, beautiful art, and sophisticated homeware. Siam Paragon and EmQuartier are major malls where tourists may find expensive goods and cutting-edge designs.

Eco-Friendly Souvenirs

As global awareness of sustainability develops, so does the desire for eco-friendly gifts. Thailand has responded to this trend by producing products produced from sustainable materials, such as bamboo, organic cotton, and recycled materials. These things not only make meaningful keepsakes but also contribute to supporting local communities and the environment.

While shopping for souvenirs, it's crucial for travelers to be culturally sensitive and knowledgeable. Some artifacts could contain religious or cultural importance, and it's crucial to understand their meaning before acquiring or displaying them. Additionally, engaging in courteous negotiating and knowing the importance of craftsmanship can build beneficial interactions with local vendors.

Conclusion

In the field of souvenir purchasing, Thailand stands out as a treasure mine of culture, craftsmanship, and diversity. Whether one seeks traditional crafts, contemporary designs, or culinary delights, Thailand's markets, boutiques, and specialty stores provide an intriguing range of possibilities. As travelers stroll the colorful kiosks, they not only purchase gifts but also weave enduring memories of a nation that celebrates its heritage in every handmade artwork.

Tour Package Options

When arranging a vacation to Thailand, travelers have a wealth of tour package alternatives to select from, each catering to different preferences and interests. Whether you're an explorer, a culture aficionado, a beach lover, or a foodie, there's a tour package in Thailand that suits your needs.

Cultural Immersion Package
For tourists seeking a deep dive into Thailand's rich history and culture, this package provides excursions to prominent monuments such as the Grand Palace in Bangkok, ancient temples like Wat Pho and Wat Arun, and the medieval city of Ayutthaya. Enjoy traditional Thai performances, explore local markets, and indulge in spiritual experiences. This bundle provides an insight into the country's cultural heritage.

Adventure and Environment Package
Thrill-seekers and environment enthusiasts will revel in this package which includes activities like jungle trekking, elephant sanctuaries, and zip-lining through lush jungles. Discover the gorgeous landscapes of northern Thailand, tour the enchanting mountains of Chiang Mai, and even take a trip to the famous Golden Triangle where Thailand, Laos, and Myanmar converge, which we described previously.

Island Getaway Package
If sun-soaked beaches and crystal-clear oceans are what you crave, the island package is the best pick. Enjoy the white

sands and frenetic nightlife of Phuket, the laid-back attitude of Koh Lanta, or the quiet beauty of Koh Phi Phi. Snorkeling, scuba diving, and water sports are all part of the experience.

Wellness and Spa Retreat Package
For those seeking relaxation and renewal, Thailand's wellness and spa getaways are second to none. Discover the art of traditional Thai massage, practice yoga amidst quiet surroundings, and indulge in elegant spa treatments that will leave you rejuvenated and renewed.

Culinary Delights Package
Thai cuisine is known globally for its richness and variety. With this package, engage on a gastronomic tour through lively food markets, street stalls, and cookery workshops. Learn to cook authentic Thai dishes and taste the explosion of flavors that distinguish the country's culinary landscape.

Family-Friendly Package
Traveling with family? Opt for a package that caters to all ages. From interactive animal encounters to kid-friendly sites, Thailand provides a choice of activities that assure a pleasant family holiday. Visit theme parks, aquariums, and cultural centers that entertain and educate.

Luxurious Escapes Package
Indulge in the lap of luxury with this package that includes stays at magnificent resorts, private villa accommodations, and exclusive experiences. Enjoy exclusive island tours, yacht cruises, and tailored services that cater to your every taste.

Volunteer and Community Engagement Package
For socially conscious travelers, Thailand gives possibilities to give back to local communities. Participate in voluntary

projects, such as teaching English to poor children or engaging in sustainable farming methods. This package allows you to make a good difference while experiencing the warmth of Thai hospitality.

Off-the-Beaten-Path Package

For the intrepid adventurer, this package journeys into lesser-known regions of Thailand. Discover secret waterfalls, secluded communities, and unspoiled natural beauty. Trek into distant forests, mingle with indigenous tribes and experience true rural life.

Conclusion

Thailand's numerous tour package selections ensure that every traveler's preferences and aspirations are catered to. Whether you're interested in cultural immersion, adventure, relaxation, or something altogether unique, there's a package that corresponds with your desires. Be careful to research thoroughly, evaluate your interests, and prepare accordingly to get the most out of your wonderful Thai trip.

Tourist Safety Tips

While Thailand offers memorable experiences, it's crucial for travelers to consider safety during their visit. Being aware of potential risks and employing caution can help to a safe and pleasurable trip, here are tourist safety guidelines in Thailand:

Research and Planning
Before embarking on your journey, obtain knowledge about the local culture, customs, and laws. Familiarize yourself with the regions you plan to visit and investigate recent travel advisories from your government. Having a well-thought-out itinerary can help you keep organized and limit the possibility of getting lost or winding yourself in risky locations.

Health Precautions
Ensure your vaccines are up to date and consider additional injections suggested for travel to Thailand. Carry a basic medical kit containing essentials like pain relievers, antiseptics, and any prescription prescriptions you might require. Stay hydrated, be cautious with street food, and avoid swallowing tap water.

Transportation Safety
Opt for certified taxis with meters or ride-sharing services for safe transportation. Be aware of tuk-tuk drivers or motorbike taxis who might overcharge tourists. If you opt to rent a motorbike, wear a helmet and drive slowly, conforming to local traffic rules.

Avoiding Scams
Tourists are occasionally targeted by scams. Be cautious of extremely nice people offering unsolicited help or things that

appear too good to be true. Whether it's gem stores, bespoke suits, or unexpected tour offerings, research beforehand to separate respectable enterprises from fraudsters.

Street and Beach Safety
Petty theft might occur, so keep your stuff secure, especially in crowded situations. Avoid showcasing pricey jewelry or electronics. When visiting the beach, stay aware of strong currents and heed warnings from lifeguards.

Nightlife Caution
Thailand's nightlife is famed, but it's necessary to exercise caution. Stay in groups, especially at night, and avoid excessive alcohol intake. Never leave your drink unattended, as drink-spiking occurrences have been documented.

Natural and Environmental Hazards
Thailand's gorgeous landscapes can contain serious perils. If you wish to travel or explore rainforests, do so with expert guides. In some places, mosquitoes can transmit diseases, so take insect repellant. During monsoon season, be aware of flooding and landslides.

Legal Awareness
Ignorance of the law is not an excuse. Familiarize oneself with local rules and regulations. Drug possession can result in severe consequences, including long jail sentences or possibly the death penalty. Always carry adequate identification, such as a photocopy of your passport.

Emergency Contact Information
Save local emergency contact numbers, including the nearest embassy or consulate, on your phone. Consider using a local

SIM card or ensuring your phone's international roaming is activated.

Accommodation Safety
Choose reliable accommodations and safeguard your belongings in a safe or lockbox. Lock your room when you're not inside and be cautious about providing sensitive information to strangers.

Travel Insurance
It's advisable to get comprehensive travel insurance that covers medical crises, trip cancellations, and other unforeseen circumstances. Confirm that your insurance offers coverage for activities you plan to partake in, such as water sports or adventure activities.

Conclusion
Being aware, respectful of local customs, and cautious in strange situations can considerably enhance your travel experience. By following this complete safety advice, you'll be better prepared to enjoy all that Thailand has to offer while reducing potential risks.

Festival and Events

Thailand has a plethora of festivals and events throughout the year that provide travelers with an appealing insight into its local culture and way of life. From elaborate religious events to boisterous street parades, each event is a unique experience that shows the country's variety and deep-rooted beliefs.

Songkran Festival (April)
One of Thailand's most popular festivities, Songkran marks the traditional Thai New Year. Lasting for several days in mid-April, this celebration is characterized by water splashing and street parties, signifying the washing away of bad luck and starting over. Tourists can join in the excitement by engaging in water fights, visiting temples to pay obeisance, and participating in traditional festivities.

Loy Krathong Festival (November)
Also known as the Festival of Lights, Loy Krathong takes place on the full moon night of the twelfth lunar month. Participants release beautifully crafted lotus-shaped rafts, called as "krathongs," onto rivers and lakes, followed by candles and incense. The celebration symbolizes letting go of negativity and paying reverence to the water gods.

Yi Peng Lantern Festival (November)
Coinciding with Loy Krathong, the Yi Peng Lantern Festival in Chiang Mai is a riveting sight as hundreds of lanterns are released into the sky, creating a beautiful display of brilliant lights. The celebration also incorporates traditional dance performances, parades, and cultural exhibitions.

Phi Ta Khon (Ghost Festival) in Dan Sai (June/July)

This unique festival is celebrated in the small town of Dan Sai and comprises colorful parades, ornate masks, and traditional dances. Participants wear ghost masks and colorful costumes, dancing through the streets to chase away evil spirits and ensure good fortune.

Vegetarian Festival (October)

Held mostly in Phuket and Bangkok's Chinatown, the Vegetarian Festival is a nine-day celebration that exhibits the influence of Chinese culture on Thailand. Participants adopt strict vegetarian diets and commit acts of self-mortification to cleanse the body and bring good luck.

Royal Barge Procession

An event of tremendous pomp and cultural significance, the Royal Barge Procession takes place on the Chao Phraya River in Bangkok. This event shows intricately built barges, each manned by a crew in traditional costumes, rowing in synchronous harmony. The parade is an uncommon occurrence and is usually organized to celebrate significant royal occasions.

Makha Bucha Day (February)

Celebrated on the full moon of the third lunar month, Makha Bucha Day celebrates the day when 1,250 disciples spontaneously gathered to listen to Buddha's teachings. Devotees participate in lighting processions around temples, paying respects to Buddha and reflecting on his teachings.

Chiang Mai Flower Festival (February)

Held in the northern city of Chiang Mai, this festival showcases the region's immense floral splendor. The sidewalks are decked with beautiful flower displays, and parades feature colorful floats made entirely of blooms. The event gathers wildlife enthusiasts, photographers, and tourists alike.

Phuket's Old Town Festival (February)
Celebrating the history and cultural legacy of Phuket, this festival transforms the ancient Old Town area into a lively fairground. Visitors can experience traditional dances, street performances, local cuisine, and craft fairs.

National Elephant Day (March 13th)
As a nation profoundly attached to elephants, Thailand celebrates National Elephant Day to raise awareness about the conservation of these wonderful creatures. Festivities include parades, elephant-related activities, and educational events.

Conclusion
Thailand's festivals and events give travelers a kaleidoscope of experiences that reflect the country's spirituality, creativity, and sense of community. From the flamboyant water battles of Songkran to the serene beauty of Loy Krathong, each occasion gives a unique opportunity to immerse oneself in Thai culture, building lasting memories and a greater understanding of the nation's customs. Travelers looking to see Thailand beyond its tourist attractions might consider organizing their visits to coincide with these intriguing and significant celebrations.

Printed in Great Britain
by Amazon

35900218R00097